Handbook of Drug Store and Business Management

New Syllabus implemented in the year 1993
(According to the Education Regulations 1991)

ASHOK K. GUPTA
M. Pharm. (Pharmaceutics)
Head of Department, Pharmacy
Govt. Polytechnic for Women, Chandigarh

CBSPD

CBS Publishers & Distributors Pvt Ltd

New Delhi • Bengaluru • Chennai • Kochi • Kolkata • Lucknow • Mumbai
Hyderabad • Jharkhand • Nagpur • Patna • Pune • Uttarakhand

Hanbdook of Drug Store and Business Management

ISBN-13: 978-81-239-0485-6
ISBN-10: 81-239-0485-1

First Edition: 1996

Reprint: 1998, 1999, 2000, 2003, 2004, 2005, 2006, 2007, 2008, 2011, 2013, 2014, 2015, 2017, 2018, 2019, 2020, 2021, 2023, **2025**

Published by **Satish Kumar Jain** and produced by **Varun Jain** for

CBS Publishers & Distributors Pvt Ltd

4819/XI Prahlad Street, 24 Ansari Road, Daryaganj, New Delhi 110 002, India.
Ph: 011-23266838, 23289259 Website: www.cbspd.com
e-mail: delhi@cbspd.com

Corporate Office: 204 FIE, Industrial Area, Patparganj, Delhi 110 092
Ph: 011-4934 4934 Fax: 011-4934 4935
e-mail: publishing@cbspd.com; publicity@cbspd.com

Branches

- **Bengaluru:** Seema House 2975, 17th Cross, KR Road, Banasankari 2nd Stage, Bengaluru 560 070, Karnataka, India
  Ph: +91-80-26771678/79 Fax: +91-80-26771680 e-mail: bangalore@cbspd.com
- **Chennai:** 7, Subbaraya Street, Shenoy Nagar, Chennai 600 030, Tamil Nadu, India
  Ph: +91-44-26680620, 26681266 Fax: +91-44-42032115 e-mail: chennai@cbspd.com
- **Kochi:** 42/1325, 1326, Power House Road, Opp KSEB, Power House, Ernakulum Kochi 682 018, Kerala, India
  Ph: +91-484-4059061-65,67 Fax: +91-484-4059065 e-mail: kochi@cbspd.com
- **Kolkata:** 147, Hind Ceramics Compound, 1st Floor, Nilgunj Road, Belghoria, Kolkata-700056, West Bengal, India
  Ph: +033-25633055, 033-25633056 e-mail: kolkata@cbspd.com
- **Lucknow:** Basement, Khushnuma Complex, 7 Meerabai Marg (Behind Jawahar Bhawan), Lucknow-226001, UP, India
  Ph: +0522-4000032 e-mail: tiwari.lucknow@cbspd.com
- **Mumbai:** PWD Shed, Gala no 25/26, Ramchandra Bhatt Marg, Next to JJ Hospital Gate no. 2, Opp. Union Bank of India, Noorbaug, Mumbai-400009, Maharashtra, India
  Ph: 022-66661880/89 e-mail: mumbai@cbspd.com

Representatives

- Hyderabad 0-9885175004
- Jharkhand 0-9811541605
- Nagpur 0-8692091830
- Patna 0-9334159340
- Pune 0-9664372571
- Uttarakhand 0-9716462459

Printed at Glorious Printers, Jhilmil Industrial Area, Delhi, India

Preface

In the revised Education Regulation, 1991, the Pharmacy Council of India has introduced a new subject "Drug Store and Business Management". This subject is extremely important to be taught at graduate and undergraduate levels because a number of students of Pharmacy may start their own drug stores, set up their own industries or seek employment in such business organisations. Therefore, it is very important for them to have knowledge about drug store and business management.

The present book titled "Handbook of Drug Store and Business Management" has been written specially for Pharmacy students, covering all the topics mentioned in the syllabus and in a very simple language so that the students may easily understand and grasp the subject without much difficulty who do not have any previous knowledge of commerce and accountancy.

My sincere thanks are due to all those teachers and students of Pharmacy who have written numerous letters of appreciation in connection with my earlier publications on Pharmaceutics I and II and inspired me to write a book on Drug Store and Business Management. I am sure that this book will also be liked and received well by my fellow teachers and students of Pharmacy.

I am grateful to Shri S.S. Bajaj, Head of Department, Pharmacy, Govt. Polytechnic for Women, Chandigarh for his valuable suggestions and expert guidance given from time to time.

I express my sincere gratitude to Shri Satish Kumar Jain and Shri Vinod Kumar Jain for their keen interest, painstaking efforts and sparing valuable time for bringing out this book in a very short span of time.

The constructive criticism and valuable suggestions from readers of this book for improvement in future editions of the book will be appreciated and gratefully acknowledged.

May 1996 ASHOK K. GUPTA

Syllabus

Drug Store and Business Management

Theory (75 hours)

Part I : Commerce (50 hours)

1. Introduction—Trade, Industry and Commerce, Functions and sub-division of Commerce, Introduction to Elements of Economics and Management.
2. Forms of Business Organisations.
3. Channels of Distribution.
4. Drug House Management—Selection of Site, Space Lay-out and legal requirements.
   Importance and Objectives of Purchasing, selection of suppliers, credit information, tenders, contracts and price determination and legal requirements thereto.
   Codification, handling of drug stores and other hospital supplies.
5. Inventory Control—objects and importance, modern techniques like ABC, VED analysis, the lead time, inventory carrying cost, safety stock, minimum and maximum stock levels, economic order quantity, scrap and surplus disposal.
6. Sales Promotion, Market Research, Salesmanship, qualities of a salesman, Advertising and Window Display.
7. Recruitment, training, evaluation and compensation of the pharmacist.
8. Banking and Finance Service and functions of bank. Finance Planning and sources of finance.

Part II : Accountancy (25 hours)

1. Introduction of the accounting concepts and conventions, Double entry Book keeping, Different kinds of accounts.
2. Cash Book.
3. General Ledger and Trial Balance.
4. Profit and Loss Account and Balance Sheet.
5. Simple technique of analysing financial statements.
   Introduction to Budgeting.

Contents

Part I

Commerce

Part I

Commerce

1

Trade, Industry and Commerce

BUSINESS

In modern age the demands of human beings are increasing day by day and to meet these demands one has to do some kind of work to earn money, that means he will have to keep himself busy in performing business activities.

The term "business" literally means to remain busy in some kind of activity. To remain busy does not mean that a person who is busy in playing cards, watching T.V., reading novels, roaming on roads purposelessly is a busy person. Here the busy person is that who remains busy in the economic activities to get financial gain and not that person who remains busy in non-economic activities. If a person makes economic gains then and only then he will be able to meet his necessities and demands of life. So, for making profits or economic gains in our society every person is busy in doing some kind of work e.g. a doctor is busy in consulting the patients, a pharmacist is busy in dispensing the medicines, a nurse is busy in administering the medicines to the patient, a chemist is busy in collecting and distributing the medicines, a technician is busy in performing various kinds of laboratory tests, a worker is busy in the factory, a teacher is busy in teaching the class and so on. According to Thomas Evelyn "Economics is the study of man's behaviour in earning his living. To earn their livings, men enter into a wide variety of occupations concerned with the production of goods and services that are needed by the community in which they live. There are innumerable occupations and a man has to choose which one he will follow." The business activities includes all activities from production to distribution of goods and services. Industry, trade and other activities like warehousing, transport, insurance, booking and advertising etc. are all parts of business activities.

Classification of business activities

The business activities are broadly classified into two groups :

A. Industry and
B. Commerce

A. INDUSTRY

The word "industry" refers to that part of business activities which relates to growing, extraction, production, conversion, processing or fabrication of goods. The industries produce different kinds of products for different purposes which may be classified as follows :

(a) Primary products
(b) Semi-manufactured goods
(c) Manufactured goods
 (i) Capital or producer's goods
 (ii) Consumer's goods

(a) Primary products

Primary products include all the products or raw materials obtained from agriculture, forests, mines, animal husbandry and fisheries etc. The examples of primary products include wheat, rice, cotton, sugarcane, cereals, wood, metal ores, milk, fish, raw silk etc. The various raw drugs obtained from plants and animals also constitute the primary products.

(b) Semi manufactured goods

Semi-manufactured goods are those goods which are produced by one industry but cannot be consumed as such unless it is passed through another industry to undergo further manufacturing processes to obtain a finished product. For example capsule shells are manufactured in one kind of industry but filling is done in another kind of industry. Similarly pig iron, cotton yarn and pulp etc. are some of the examples of semi-manufactured goods.

(c) Manufactured goods

Manufactured goods are those goods which are ready for use by the consumers or other users. The examples of manufactured goods include cloth, shoes, sugar, paper, various medicines, machines, tools etc.

The manufactured goods are further classified as (i) capital or producer's goods, (ii) consumer's goods.

(i) Capital or producer's goods

Capital or producer's goods are those goods which are used in the process of producing some other goods. The examples of producer's goods include pig iron, store items, machine tools and machinery etc. used for manufacturing other products.

(ii) Consumer's goods

Consumer's goods are those goods which are ready to use by the consumers and require no further processing. The examples of consumer's goods include drugs such as tablets, capsules, syrups, injections etc.; cloth, shoes, soap, T.V., fridge, washing machine etc.

Classification of industries

According to the types of goods produced the industries are classified as follows :

1. Genetic industries
2. Extractive industries

3. Manufacturing industries
4. Construction industries

Chart showing classification of industries

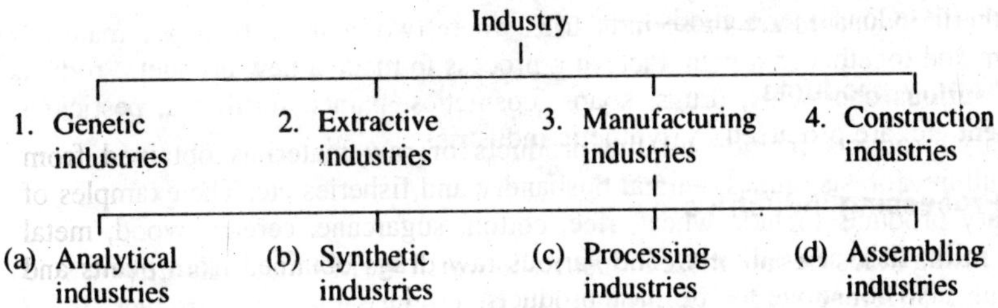

1. Genetic industries

The word genetic is derived from the term "genetics" which means heredity. It means genetic industries are concerned with the reproduction or multiplication of plants, animals and birds. The examples of genetic industries include plant breeding nurseries, cattle breeding farms, poultry farms and fish hatcheries.

2. Extractive industries

Extractive industries are those industries which are concerned with extraction or drawing out the products from natural sources such as soil, air or water. The products so obtained are generally used by other industries producing finished goods. Extractive industries include agriculture, mining, oil exploration, forestry, fishing etc.

3. Manufacturing industries

Manufacturing industries are those industries which are engaged in the production of goods. Here the raw materials or semi-manufactured products are converted into finished goods i.e. capital goods or consumer's goods. Generally the goods supplied by the extractive industries are used as a raw material for manufacturing industries. For example pharmaceutical, textile, jute, sugar, cement, engineering and steel industries are some of the examples of manufacturing industries which alter the form of raw materials to make them more useful to the consumers. Manufacturing industries may be further sub-divided as follows :

(a) Analytical industries
(b) Synthetic industries
(c) Processing industries
(d) Assembling industries

(a) Analytical industries

Analytical industries are those industries which are engaged in the analysis of one kind of basic material and after separating a number of products are obtained from the same material. For example crude oil is extracted from beneath the earth which is subjected to fractional distillation. After fractional distillation it is separated into petrol, diesel, kerosene, gasoline and lubricating oil etc.

(b) Synthetic industries

Synthetic industries are those industries where two or more than two materials are mixed together in a manufacturing process to make a new product. Products like various chemicals, drugs, soaps, cosmetics, paints, fertilizers, pesticides, cement etc. are produced by synthetic industries.

(c) Processing industries

Processing industries are those industries in which the raw materials are processed through different stages of production to produce the final product. In the processing industries the analytical and synthetic methods may also be used. Drugs and pharmaceutical industries, paper, textile, sugar and steel industries are some of the examples of processing industries.

(d) Assembling industries

Assembling industries are those industries where the parts or components are assembled to make a useful product. The parts or components required in assembling may be produced by the assembling industry itself or obtained from other industries engaged in the manufacture of required components. Such industries are known as ancillary industries. For example production of cars, scooters, watches, television, radio, computers, X-ray machines, E.C.G. machines etc. are the typical examples of assembling industries.

4. Construction industries

Construction industries are those industries which are engaged in the construction of roads, buildings, canals, bridges, dams etc. The products of other manufacturing industries such as iron, cement, bricks, stones, marble, wood, glass, rubber etc. are used by the construction industries. Construction industries are extremely important and useful for the economic development of any nation.

B. COMMERCE

The main object of an industry is to produce goods and services for the satisfaction of human wants whereas commerce is concerned with the distribution of goods to the consumers and users according to their tastes, needs and conveniences. It includes all those activities which are related to the transfer of goods from the place of production to the ultimate consumers. Thus commerce serves as a valuable link between the producer and the consumer. Now a days commerce consists of a complex well developed system of transport, insurance, warehousing and other similar activities which facilitate trade.

In the words of Evelyn Thomas "Commercial occupations deal with the buying and selling of goods, the exchange of commodities and the distribution of the finished products."

Production is done at certain places but consumers are scattered far and wide.

Their requirements cannot be met only with the centralisation of supply of goods at a place. The commercial activities help in the distribution of goods to the consumers and users through markets situated at different places. Thus consumers and other users can obtain their requirements wherever they need, whenever they need and the quantities in which they need. In this way the wheels of commerce move on and on to render the exchange of goods as smooth as possible and to deploy the goods all over the market and make them available to the consumers.

James Stephenson defined commerce as "Commerce embraces all those processes which help to break the barrier between producers and consumers. It is the sum total of those processes which are engaged in the removal of hindrances of persons (trade), place (transport and insurance) and time (warehousing) in the exchange (banking) of commodities."

Components/subdivisions of commerce

Commerce has the following components/subdivisions :

1. Trade and
2. Aids to trade.

1. Trade

Trade means buying and selling of goods. A trader purchases goods to be sold to other traders or consumers at a profit. Generally he buys those goods which are in demand or which are likely to find response in the market. He may hold them in the store and sell them at an appropriate time when he will be able to get good margin of profit.

Since the goods are manufactured at far off places but are required by the consumers all cver the world, the producer cannot supply the goods individually to all the consumers. So he appoints some dealers or distributors for the distribution of goods known as traders. Thus traders act as intermediaries between producers and consumers. They buy the goods at most competitive prices and sell at higher prices depending on the trends of demand in the market. Sometimes they may get good margin of profit but sometimes they may go in losses. Trade, thus refers to buying, selling, transfer or exchange of goods or services for money or money's worth.

Classification of trade

The trade is generally classified into following categories :

1. Internal trade
2. International trade

1. Internal trade

Internal trade is also known as home trade because buying and selling is done within the boundaries of the country which may be (a) local trade i.e. the goods are purchased and sold at a particular place; (b) state trade i.e. the goods are traded only in a particular state; (c) interstate trade i.e. the goods are bought and sold from one state to another state. The payments involved in trading are made in nation's own currency directly or through the banking system. Internal trade may be further sub-classified as follows :

(i) Wholesale trade and
(ii) Retail trade.

(i) Wholesale trade

In wholesale trade the wholesalers buy the goods in large quantities directly from the manufacturers and sell them in smaller quantities to retailers who are in direct contact with the consumers. Thus wholesalers serve as a link between the manufacturers and retailers.

(ii) Retail trade

When the goods are distributed in small quantities to the consumers it is known as retail trade. Retailing is the final stage in distribution of goods and involves direct selling to the ultimate consumers. The persons who deal in retail sale of goods are known as retailers. Retail trade may be conducted through shops, departmental stores, multiple shops, co-operative stores, super bazars, vendors etc. A retailer is a direct link between manufacturer and/or wholesaler and consumer.

2. International trade

International trade is also known as foreign trade or external trade. When the goods or services are exchanged between two or more than two countries then it is known as foreign trade. Exchange of goods takes place by making the payments in the currency of the country concerned called foreign exchange. Movement of goods is done through international system of transport.

Foreign trade plays a vital role in the economic development of a country. Through imports a country is enabled to obtain plant, machinery and equipment, components, raw materials and technical know-how which are extremely important for the economic development of any country specially for the under-developed and developing countries if they wish to remove poverty from their countries.

Classification of foreign trade

Foreign trade may be further classified as follows :

(i) Import trade
(ii) Export trade
(iii) Entrepot trade

(i) Import trade

When the trader brings the goods from foreign countries to his own country it is known as import trade. For example when India brings goods from Japan, USA, or any other country it is known as import trade.

(ii) Export trade

When the goods of one country are sold to other countries it is known as export trade. For example India sells goods like drugs, cloth, readymade garments, tea, coffee etc. to other countries. It is known as export trade.

(iii) Entrepot trade

Entrepot trade is also known as re-export trade. It involves the import of foreign goods of one country with the idea of exporting the same to other countries and making profit in the process. For example if a trader of India imports goods from Singapore, Japan and China and sells the same to any other country with a margin of profit it is known as entrepot trade.

2. Aids to trade or functions of commerce or branches of commerce

Various branches of commerce are given below :

(i) Transport
(ii) Warehousing
(iii) Banking
(iv) Insurance
(v) Packaging
(vi) Advertising and publicity.

(i) Transport

Transport removes obstacle of place. It is the process of carrying goods and persons from one place to another. It is concerned with carrying the goods from the places of production to the places of their consumption. Apart from increasing the mobility of goods, workers and capital it also helps in stabilizing the prices. Transport removes obstacle of place as the goods are removed from the place of production to the place of its consumption. Therefore a well knit transport system plays a very important role in the economic development, social welfare and political integration of any country.

Like other industries, pharmaceutical industries are situated at selective places depending on the availability of raw materials, labour, easy transportation and favourable climatic conditions. After production the drugs must reach to the consumers in the shortest possible time because certain drugs get deteriorated with passage of time. Thus suitable transportation facilities are essential for the distribution of drugs as well as procuring of raw materials and other essential items within a reasonable time.

There are various modes of transport available for moving the goods, drugs and pharmaceuticals from one place to another which include road, rail, air, water, pipeline transport etc. Out of all these modes of transport, railways are considered as the most effective means of movement of goods because :

(a) It is cheaper for bulky goods to be carried over long distances.
(b) The goods are more safe than in road transport since they are carried in covered wagons and not in make-shift arrangements like in road transport.

(c) Since the railways are government controlled so the freights are less.

(ii) Warehousing (storage)

Warehousing removes the hindrance of time. Warehouses are the places where goods are stored.

Storage is the process of keeping, holding and preserving the goods which are to be used at a later stage. When this process is done at a large scale and in a specialized manner it is termed as warehousing. The basic idea of storage is to keep the goods in proper conditions, to make the goods available as and when required and to ensure continuous and unrestricted supply of goods in the market.

Need and Importance of Storage

1. Now a days the goods are continuously produced. All the goods are not immediately sold so the unsold goods will have to be stored.
2. Storage of raw materials is necessary to ensure uninterrupted production.
3. Many drugs are used in a particular season but they are produced throughout the year so they will have to be stored for sale as and when required.
4. Storage is necessary to take the advantage of bulk buying.
5. It is done in anticipation of demand.
6. Certain goods which can get higher prices in future are stored for a longer period. For this purpose perishable goods like fruits, vegetables etc. can be stored in cold storage.
7. Storage is necessary for wholesalers as well as retailers for regular supply to the consumers.

Thus from the above discussion it is clear that warehouses remove hindrance of time in trade by storing the goods which may be supplied to the consumers as and when required.

(iii) Banking

Hindrance of finance is removed by banking. Finance or capital is the life blood of any business. Without finance it is not possible to run any marketing activity. A large amount of money is required for the production and marketing of goods and services. Finance is needed for the purchase of machinery, raw materials, carrying production operations, meeting transportation, storage and insurance expenses. The wholesalers and retailers also need finance for purchasing, storing, giving credit to their customers and for meeting day to day expenses.

The finance can be raised from own sources, commercial banks, shares, debentures, financial institutions, trade creditors etc. The banks provide the facilities of overdraft, cash credits, discounting of the bills of exchange and a lot of other services to the customers thus removing the hindrance of finance in trade.

(iv) Insurance

Insurance removes the hindrance of risks. In marketing process many kinds of risks are involved at every stage. From the time of production to the time of disbursement of goods to the actual consumer they are exposed to many risks on account of unavoidable circumstances e.g. fire, accidents, theft, storm, floods, earthquake, price reduction, changes in demand and supply conditions, non-recovery of credit sales, dishonesty of employees and partner(s), strikes, lockouts and pilferage etc.

Risks due to natural calamities like pests, rain, hailstorm, lightning, fire, floods, drought, earthquakes etc. are the most destructive type of risks and can be covered by insurance.

Losses due to dishonesty, strikes, lockouts and pilferage can be minimised by developing cordial relations and understanding between employers and employees.

Risks due to price reduction, changes in demand and supply conditions, non-recovery of credit sales and other risks can be minimised by thorough analysis of market trend, government policies and reputation of creditors. Outstanding payments may be collected by improving methods of collection or by adopting other suitable means of collection.

All the above mentioned risks are covered by insurance companies provided the necessary insurance has been done and premiums have been regularly paid. An insurance company performs a useful service by compensating the traders for the losses due to fire, theft, flood or other natural calamities etc. Thus insurance companies protect the traders from the fear of loss of goods. The insurance companies charge a nominal insurance premium for the risks covered.

There are various types of insurance policies to cover the risk of losses. For example life insurance policy covers the risk of life, fire insurance policy covers the risk of losses due to fire, marine insurance policy covers the risk of loss or damage during shipment of goods or passengers.

(v) Packaging

Packaging removes the risk of spoilage. Packaging is the process by which the pharmaceuticals are suitably packed so that they retain their therapeutic effectiveness from the time of their packaging till they are consumed. Packaging may be defined as the art and science which involves preparing the articles for transport, storage, display and use. An utmost care might have been taken during the formulation of any preparation but if it is not packaged properly the whole aim may be lost. Different shapes and sizes of containers made from different materials are used for packing different types of formulations. Therefore a careful consideration must be given for the selection of packaging material. Properly packaged materials will be protected from deterioration and spoilage. Thus the risk involved due to spoilage will be removed.

(vi) Advertising and publicity

Advertising and publicity removes the hindrance of knowledge or information gap about the availability and uses of goods between traders and consumers. The main object of advertisement is to create demand and to increase the sales. The various methods used for advertisement are : T.V., radio, newspapers, magazines, wall posters, pamphlets, free samples, trade fairs, exhibitions, balloons and window display etc.

Thus trade, transport, warehousing, banking, insurance etc. are the different branches of commerce.

ELEMENT OF ECONOMICS

In order to study the elements of economics, it becomes necessary to understand what economics is. Economics is a social science which deals with the economic problems of an individual. It also deals with the proper use and allocation of resources for the achievement of various human wants and maintenance of growth with stability.

With the overall growth of industry and increased standard of living the human wants are also increasing day by day. No doubt the human wants are unlimited but the financial resources to satisfy them are limited. Therefore the desires will have to be satisfied with limited resources. To earn money every person is engaged in some kind of economic activities e.g. business, profession or employment. A businessman earns profits, a doctor charges fee for his services and an employee gets salaries from the employer, a labourer gets wages from his master etc.

There are some non-economic activities which are related to social, psychological and religious sentiments. The examples of such activities are a housewife looking after the household, a person playing cards, a person engaged in social activities etc. Such non-economic activities do not generate any income or profit.

In order to study the elements of economics the following aspects of economics may be taken into consideration :

1. Economic activities
2. Economic system.

1. Economic activities

To satisfy the various needs with limited resources the following economics can be adopted :

(i) In an industrial house drug store economy can be adopted in the purchase of raw materials/drugs i.e. only the required raw materials and that too according to economic order quantity are purchased. The limited number of technical and non-technical persons are employed.

(ii) Only those types of products and services are produced which are economical and profitable.

(iii) Buying and selling of goods and services should be done economically i.e. at the time of buying any product minimum rate should be quoted but at the time of selling a product it must be sold by taking into consideration the margin of profit.

2. Economic system

An economic system denotes the economic relationships which arise in the community from the organisation or mode of production and distribution. The economic system should be simple and easy for human beings to satisfy their wants but it all depends on the kind of economic system which is adopted by a particular country that how the resources are allocated, prices are fixed etc.

TYPES OF ECONOMIC SYSTEMS

There are three economic systems :

(a) Capitalist system
(b) Socialist system
(c) Mixed economy

(a) Capitalist system

According to capitalist system there is freedom of every kind. The producers are free to acquire any property and to produce any product. The consumers are free to use any product and in any amount to satisfy their wants. They are also at liberty to spend their income in any way they like. According to this system the means of production and distribution are generally in the hands of private owners who operate them to earn profits. In this system the role of government is to protect the producers and consumers so as to avoid unhealthy competition among producers and to provide essential services to the public economically.

(b) Social system

According to this system the large and basic industries are owned and controlled by the government. Even the distribution is also controlled by the government.

(c) Mixed economy

In mixed economy the activities of both the systems i.e. capitalist system and social system are used. It means some economic activities are controlled by the government and some economic activities are kept open for the public. The advantages of capitalist system include better economic development, increased production and improvement in science and technology sphere. The advantages of socialist system include reduction of inequality of income, large and basic industries come under the purview of the government and there is fair distribution of consumer goods.

MANAGEMENT

Management is the process of conducting and managing the various business activities. Every business organisation, whether a drug store, hospital pharmacy, industry or any other organisation, has its own management. Without sound and experienced management it is not possible to run the business effectively. When the principles and practices of management are applied to pharmaceutical industry and drug stores, it is known as "Pharmaceutical Management".

There a number of definitions of management given by different authors but according to George R. Terry, "Management is a distinct process consisting of planning, organising, activating and controlling performed to determine and accomplish the objectives of the organisation by the use of human beings and other resources."

Management is an art and science of performing the different activities of the organisation. It is an art of getting the things done through and by the people working in the organisation. It is also a function of working with people and co-ordinating their efforts so as to accomplish the objectives of the organisation. Management is a science because it proves, predicts, defines, measures and utilizes knowledge.

To accomplish certain goals of the organisation the different activities are looked after and controlled by senior persons individually known as "Managers". In other words, a manager is a person who performs the managerial functions of planning, organising, staffing, controlling and directing.

Elements of management or functions of management

The followings are the main elements or functions of management :

1. Planning
2. Organising
3. Staffing
4. Directing
5. Controlling
6. Co-ordination

1. Planning

One of the most important function of a management is to give a serious thought about planning because all the other functions of management depend on planning.

Before starting any hospital pharmacy it is very important to plan the things. Without sound planning it is very difficult to achieve the desired aims. Therefore a sound thinking must be given that what is to be done, when and where it is to be done and how it is to be done according to the funds available. What type of products are to be formulated, type of building and equipment required. The number of pharmacists, skilled and lay personnels required, their salary etc. Provisions for the supply of good quality of raw materials and finished products and facilities for the testing of these materials.

?. Organising

"An organisation may be defined as the arrangement of persons in any field so that they act as one body and work together to fulfill the common goal." Better the organisation better would be the achievement of the common objectives. Similarly loose organisation would lead to unhappy and serious results. Therefore it is the most important task of the management to build a strong organisational structure and to fit the right person in the right place in order to achieve the goals efficiently and economically.

3. Staffing

It is the function of the management that the right persons are selected for specific kind of job. The staffing functions involve recruitment, selection, training, development, compensation, dismissal etc.

The staff of hospital pharmacy comprises of registered pharmacists, skilled persons, lay persons and clerical staff. All the staff members must know their duties and place of work. They should discharge their duties and responsibilities in the best way because all of them are engaged in the health care of the patient is one way or the other. All the employees must have good relations with both intra- and inter-departmental employees.

4. Directing

After planning, organising and staffing it is in the foremost function of the management to give proper direction to its employees to work efficiently and effectively to fulfill the objectives of the organisation. To give proper direction and command to its employees, a manager must be in a position to command or control a group of persons. For this purpose he must have leadership qualities and must be able to influence, motivate and persuade the people.

5. Controlling

The manager should have full control on the workers working under him, that means everything is done according to the rules and instructions issued to them. At the same time there should not be undue interference in their work which is likely to lose all initiative and enthusiasm to do work sincerely and honestly.

6. Co-ordination

Co-ordination means that all the working units as well as employees/workers of the organisation work in complete harmony to fulfill the goals of the organisation. The management should watch carefully that everybody in the organisation understands the objectives of the organisation and work in full co-ordination with others to achieve the business objectives.

REVISION QUESTIONS

(A) Multiple choice questions

Select the right answer and put the correct word in the respective squares given below :

1. Business means :
   (a) Trade and commerce　　(b) Buying and selling of goods
   (c) Commerce　　(d) Industry and commerce
2. Business is concerned with :
   (a) Economic activity　　(b) Non-economic activity
   (c) Both (a) and (b)　　(d) None of the above

3. Business activities include :
   (a) Industry and commerce (b) Banking and finance
   (c) None of the above
4. Transport removes the hindrance of :
   (a) Persons (b) Time
   (c) Place (d) None of the above
5. Banking removes the hindrance of :
   (a) Place (b) Time
   (c) Risk (d) Finance
6. Warehousing removes the hindrance of :
   (a) Time (b) Place
   (c) Persons (d) None of the above
7. Insurance removes the hindrance of :
   (a) Persons (b) Time
   (c) Risk (d) Spoilage
8. Trade between two countries is known as :
   (a) Import (b) Export
   (c) Foreign trade (d) Regional trade
9. To bring goods from another country to one's own country is known as :
   (a) Import (b) Export
   (c) Entreport (d) None of the above
10. Buying and selling of goods so as to make profit is known as :
   (a) Trade (b) Commerce
   (c) None of the above

1	2	3	4	5	6	7	8	9	10

(B) Match the items of column I with the appropriate items of column II

Column I	Column II
(a) Hindrance of time is removed by	(i) Banking
(b) Hindrance of risk is removed by	(ii) Packaging
(c) Hindrance of finance is removed by	(iii) Warehousing
(d) Hindrance of spoilage is removed by	(iv) Import
(e) To bring goods from one country to another country is known as	(v) Insurance
(f) Hindrance of place is removed by	(vi) Transport

a	b	c	d	e	f

(C) Short answer type questions

(a) Define the following terms :

(i) Trade (ii) Industry
(iii) Commerce (iv) Internal trade
(v) External trade (vi) Management
(vii) Synthetic industry (viii) Processing industry

(b) Differentiate between :

(i) Heavy industry and light industry
(ii) Consumer goods and producer goods
(iii) Internal trade and external trade

(D) Long answer type questions

1. Explain the term 'industry' and discuss various kinds of products produced by industries.
2. What do you understand from the term 'industry'? Classify and explain various types of industries.
3. Explain various components or subdivision of commerce.
4. Write shore notes on the following :
   (i) Internal trade (ii) External trade
   (iii) Hindrance of finance
5. Discuss various branches of commerce and explain how they are helpful to trade.
6. Explain various hindrances which arises in trade and discuss how these hindrances can be removed.
7. What do you understand from the term 'Management'? Explain various elements or functions of management.

Answers

(A)

1	2	3	4	5	6	7	8	9	10
d	a	a	c	d	a	c	c	a	a

(B)

a	b	c	d	e	f
(iii)	(v)	(i)	(ii)	(iv)	(vi)

2

Forms of Business Organisations

The term "business" literally means to keep oneself busy and a person remains busy to earn or gain something. A businessman remains busy to earn profits through production and exchange of goods and/or services. It includes all kinds of activities of industry, trade and commerce like manufacturing, packaging, warehousing, transporting, selling etc. with the sole aim of earning profits. Business may be run by an individual person or a group of individuals. When the business is handled by a group of persons it is known as business organisation. A business organisation is also known as business undertaking, business firm, business enterprise or business concern.

According to Wheeler a business undertaking is "a concern, company, or enterprise which buys and sells, is owned by one person or a group of persons and is managed under a specific set of operating policies." It is the outcome of the efforts of one or more entrepreneurs who pool their resources and co-ordinate their activities to carry on the business activities.

Characteristics of business organisations

1. The mains aim of any kind of business organisation is to earn profits at least to get back more than the amount originally invested by them in carrying on the business activities.
2. All business organisations are engaged in the production or sale of goods or services for money or money's worth.
3. The business organisations are supposed to carry on the business activities continuously and regularly.
4. All business organisations have the social responsibilities to provide the goods and services to the consumers and other user departments in the form they like, at the places they want, in the quantities the require, at the time they need and at the prices they can afford.
5. All business organisations are exposed to risk of natural calamities, labour problems, bad debits, changes in policies, demand, styles and fashions etc.

FORMS OF BUSINESS ORGANISATIONS

On the basis of ownership the various forms of business organisations are given below :

A. Private enterprises
   (i) Sole proprietorship

(ii) Joint Hindu family firm
(iii) Partnership firm
(iv) Joint stock company
(v) Co-operative societies

B. State enterprises or public enterprises
(i) Departmental organisations
(ii) Public corporations
(iii) Government company

Chart showing ownership forms of business organisations

Ownership forms of business organisations

Private enterprises	Public/state enterprises
(i) Sole proprietorship	(i) Departmental organisations
(ii) Partnership firm	(ii) Public corporations
(iii) Joint Hindu family firm	(iii) Government company
(iv) Joint stock company	
(v) Co-operative societies	

A. Private enterprises

(i) Sole proprietorship

When an individual owns and manages a business organisation it is called sole proprietorship, sole tradership or one men business organisation. In this form of business organisation the enterprise is owned and controlled by a single person. He invests his own or borrowed capital, manages and controls the business himself, bears all the risks of the business all alone and takes himself all the decisions regarding business. According to S.R. Davar, "The sole trader is a person who carries on business of his own i.e. without the assistance of a partner. He brings in his own capital and uses all his labour."

Sole proprietorship is the simplest and oldest form of business organisation. Any person who has the aptitude for business and is able to arrange the finance can start the sole proprietorship organisation. He may choose to start any kind of business with or without undergoing the legal formalities. Routine kind of shops may be started without much legal formalities but for starting a wholesale or retail sale drug store various kinds of legal formalities will have to be completed. He may run the business alone with his own skills or may employ skilled/technical person(s) to run the business. Sole proprietorship organisation is most popular for starting a drug store because it can be started individually with small finance.

Advantages

1. It is simple and easy to start.
2. It can be started even with meager finance from his personal resources or borrowed from his friends and relatives.
3. Capital can be increased or decreased at his will.

4. The owner has the complete control of the business. Therefore, he can take any kind of decision.
5. The secrecy of the business can be maintained.
6. He is free to employ any number of persons and terminate the services of any person according to his will.
7. Since he is the sole recipient of all the profits so he will try to put hard labour to earn maximum profits.
8. The sole proprietor will have intimate contacts with customers. Therefore, he can better understand their tastes, attitudes, habits and can come to known their difficulties, complaints and opinions because he comes in personal contacts with the customers.
9. The overhead cost of management is relatively less since the business is looked after by the proprietor himself, his relatives or by sincere and faithful employees.
10. The sole trader can change the business or wind up the business according to his own will without involving legal formalities.
11. It encourages self-employment therefore most suitable for professionally qualified persons. Hence most of the pharmacists run sole proprietorship drug stores.

Disadvantages

1. Sole trader may not be in a position to expand the business because of limited financial resources.
2. Since he is the sole person to handle all the activities of the business for which he may not have the expertise, for smooth running of business he will have to employ or avail the services of experts or professionals.
3. Sole tradership is limited to small business only.
4. There is a limited scope for expansion due to limited capital as well as limited manpower.
5. Being sole person to look after the business, he may not be in a position to spare time for bringing the items to his establishment or for attending the social activities. For such activities he may have to close the shop for certain period of time or to depend on the suppliers and workers.
6. The business may come to a stand still due to long illness, disability or death of the proprietor unless his heirs or successors too have the same capacity and ability to run the business.

Though sole proprietorship or one man business has certain limitations or disadvantages, even then this is the best form of business organisation in the world provided the proprietor is intelligent enough to handle all the activities of the business himself.

(ii) Joint Hindu family firm

When the property is inherited by a Hindu from his father, grandfather and great-grandfather it is known as ancestral property. Son, grandson and great-grandson become joint owners of the property by reason of their birth in the family. Thus three successive generations can simultaneously inherit the ancestral property. This interest in inheritance is called coparcenary interest and three generations next to the holder of the property in unbroken male line constitute a coparcenary. After the death of holder of property his business becomes the jointly owned business of the living male issues who constitute the coparcenary and are known as coparcenars. When the coparcenars look after their business it becomes the joint Hindu family business and the firm is known as joint Hindu family firm. Generally in a joint Hindu family firms the senior most male member of the family known as the "Karta" looks after the affairs of the joint Hindu family business.

Advantages

The joint Hindu family firm has the following advantages :

1. The business remains stable and in existence even due to disability or death of any member of the family.
2. All the members of the family can be absorbed/employed in the organisation. Hence no need to seek employment by the members of the family somewhere else. Even the uneducated or inexperienced members can be absorbed.
3. The business will be well organised and controlled since the members of the family are looking after the business.
4. Secrecy of the business will be maintained as no outsider will interfere in the business.
5. There is no maximum limit of members of the family to be absorbed in the organisation as for other kinds of business organisations if the number of members exceed more than 20 the firm will have to be registered itself with the registrar of companies (Section 11 of the Companies Act, 1956).
6. The profits will be divided among the members of the family only.

Disadvantages

1. Differences may arise if any member of the family starts deceiving other members or does not take interest in the affairs of the business.
2. Quarrels may start on the division of the property.
3. Relatively limited financial resources.
4. Continuity of the firm depends on the continuity of the joint family itself.

(iii) Partnership firm

When two or more than two persons join together to contribute money and/or labour or skill and share the profits and losses among themselves are individually known as partners and collectively known as firm. According to Indian Partnership Act, 1932 partnership is defined as the relation between persons who have agreed to share the profits of a business carried on by all or any of them acting for all. According to Indian Contract Act, the partnership is defined as the relationship which exists between persons, who have agreed to combine their property, labour or skill in some business and to share the profits thereof between them.

According to Section 11 of the Companies Act, 1956 up to a maximum of twenty persons (ten in case of banking business) can join together to share any profit made by the firm.

The limitations and deficiencies of sole proprietor such as limited financial resources, limited managerial skills, limited manpower and limited scope to bear the business risks all alone led to the formation of partnership form of business organisation. Partnership is formed on the basis of an agreement between the concerned partners. The partnership agreement may be oral or written. The written document of partnership is known as "Partnership Deed" which is made in the court of law. The partners cannot transfer their shares to outsiders without the written consent of other partner(s). The profits and losses of the firm will be divided among the partners in the ratio agreed upon at the time of formation of partnership firm.

Advantages

1. It is easy to form a partnership firm. Any two or more than two like-minded persons can join together to start the firm. An oral or written agreement is enough to start the partnership firm. There are no complicated legal formalities regarding the formation of such firm.
2. The firm may or may not get itself registered with the registrar of companies according to Partnership Act, 1932.
3. The partners may pool their resources to collect enough funds for the smooth running of the business. If the need arises new partners can be admitted in the firm to secure more capital. Moreover for expansion purposes the funds can be raised from outside sources.
4. The different activities of the business can be administered by the appropriate and qualified partner in that particular line.
5. Any kind of decision can be taken promptly because the partners can meet at a short notice.
6. The secrecy of the business can be maintained as the partnership firms are not supposed to publish its accounts as in the case of Joint Stock Company.
7. If all the partners take full interest in the business then there are greater chances of growth and expansion of the business because of large capital, division of work, better administration, division of risks etc.
8. In case of losses in business the risks are shared by all the partners.
9. If need arises the business can be dissolved by giving 14 days notice to other partners. No regal formalities are required for this purpose.
10. If the partners are sincere and hard working the profits of the firm will increase and ultimately each partner will get more amount of profit.

Disadvantages

1. Large scale business may not be possible to run in a partnership firm

because of limited resources as the number of partners in a partnership firm cannot exceed 20 which put a limit to raise the capital for large scale operations.

2. Generally the partnership firms do not last for a long time due to misunderstandings and lack of mutual co-operation among the partners. In such cases the partnership leads to dissolution of the firm.
3. If any partner withdraws his partnership by giving a short notice then in certain cases the firm may have to be dissolved.
4. No partner can transfer his capital or interest in the firm to outsiders without the consent of all the partners.
5. A dishonest and incompetent partner may land the firm in difficult position by leaking the secrets of the firm or by making complaints to the authorities.
6. Public in general do not have much faith in partnership firms because their accounts are kept a closely guarded secrets. Moreover no body knows when the firm will be dissolved hence the people hesitate to give the things on credit to such firms.
7. The liabilities of the partners are unlimited. If the firm goes into losses the creditors can recover their dues even from the private property of partners. This is the main drawback of partnership firms.

Kinds of partners

The partners of a partnership firm may be of following types :

(a) Active or working partner
(b) Sleeping or inactive partner
(c) Nominal partner.
(d) Partner in profits only
(e) Secret partner
(f) Partner by estoppel
(g) Partner by holding out
(h) Minor as a partner.

(a) Active or working partner

Active or working partner is that partner who takes active part in the management as well as in the day to day functioning of the business. The active partner also contributes capital to the firm. He may be given certain amount of remuneration for his services depending on the agreement. In the real sense he is the full-fledged partner of the firm.

(b) Sleeping or inactive partner

Some of the persons merely contribute the capital to the firm but do not take any active part in the conduct of business of the firm. Such partners are known as sleeping or inactive partners. They share the profits and losses of the firm and have a voice in the management but their relationship with the firm is not disclosed to the public.

(c) Nominal partner

Nominal partner is that partner who neither contributes capital nor takes active part in the conduct of business of the firm but only lends his name and reputation for the benefit of the firm. A nominal partner does not share the profits of the business but he is liable to outsiders for the debts of the firm.

(d) Partner in profits only

Partner in profits only is that partner who contributes money with the idea of getting share in the profits only and does not share the losses of the firm but is fully liable to the creditors of the firm. As a rule such a partner has no voice in the management of the business. The object of having such a partner in the firm is to make use of his money and goodwill.

(e) Secret partner

A secret partner is that partner who does not want to be known as partner of the firm to the outsiders, though in reality he is a partner. Such a partner can take part in the conduct of business of the firm. However, he is liable to outsiders like any other partner of the firm.

(f) Partner by estoppel

Partner by estoppel is that person who has neither contributed any capital to firm nor takes part in the management of the firm but behaves or talks to the outsiders in such a manner that he creates an impression in their minds that he is a partner of the firm. With this impression, the third parties may grant credit to the firm whereas in reality such a person is not a partner in that firm. Because he has given wrong impressions of being partner of the firm so he will be liable for the debts of the firm to the third parties who might have entered into contract with the firm.

(g) Partner by holding out

When a person is declared as a partner of the firm in written or spoken words by others and the concerned person does not deny or contradict the partnership relationship, then he is considered as a partner of the firm and becomes liable to such third parties who deal with the firm in the belief that he is a partner of that firm. Such a person is known as partner by holding out and is not entitled to any profit.

(h) Minor as a partner

A person below the age of 18 years is considered as minor. According to law a minor is not competent to contract therefore he cannot become a partner in a partnership firm, however he can be admitted as a partner provided all other partners agree to it. He is entitled to the share in the profits and property of the firm. So long he remains a minor his liabilities remain limited to the extent of his share in the profits and property of the firm.

Kinds of partnership

Partnership is of two types :

(a) General partnership
(b) Limited partnership

(a) General partnership

In a general partnership the liabilities of all the partners are unlimited. It means if the assets of the firm are not sufficient to pay off the dues then the creditors of the firm can realise their dues in full by attaching the private property of the partners. All partners of a general partnership firm have the authority to participate in the management of business of the firm.

(b) Limited partnership

Due to the major drawback of general partnership that all the partners have unlimited liability the partners are not willing to invest heavy capitals in the firm but if their liabilities are limited only to the extent of their individual share in the capital of the firm then they would willingly become the partners of the firm. The main features of the limited partnership are that :

(a) A limited partnership consists of two types of partners i.e. general partners and limited or special partners. The liability of general partners is unlimited whereas the liability of limited or special partners is limited to their share of capital in the firm.
(b) In a limited partnership at least one partner should be a general partner and others may be limited or special partners.
(c) A limited partner simply invested his money in the firm, he does not have any authority to take part in the management of business of the firm but he can check the books of accounts for his information.
(d) The death or bankruptcy of a special partner will not effect the existence of the firm in any way. Therefore a limited partnership is more stable than a general partnership firm.

According to Indian Partnership Act only the general partnership firms can be formed and no limited partnership firm can be formed with limited liability in this country.

(IV) Joint Stock Company

Since the sole proprietorship and partnership forms of business organisation suffer from many limitations like limited financial resources, limited managerial ability, doubtful continuity and unlimited liability etc., therefore, taking into consideration all these limitations and changing trends of modern development in the fields of production, transport, communication and contribution, it became necessary to find out a new kind of business organisation which will meet all the requirements of modern development specially the finances required for large scale business. Therefore a form of business organisation capable of mobilising larger amount of capital with the provision of limited liability and efficient management came into existence known as joint stock company.

Joint stock company comes into existence where a number of persons who are unknown to each other join together to contribute and invest their money in a common enterprise. Such investors are known as share holders. The number of share holders may be increased indefinitely to collect the required amount of capital. The persons who contribute for the investment become members of the company thus the capital of the company is held jointly by the shareholders, that is why it is known as joint stock company. The shares of the company are transferable although the right to transfer them is often more or less restricted.

The existence of the company is affected by entering the new members or leaving the existing members of the company. In case of failure of company, the liability of each investor for the debt of the company is limited to the amount of his original investment in the company.

There are a number of definitions of company but according to Justice Lindley, "A company is an association of many persons who contribute money or money's worth to a common stock and employ it for a common purpose. The common stock so contributed is denoted in money and is capital of the company. The persons who contribute it or to whom it belongs are members. The proportions of capital to which each member is entitled is his share. Shares are always transferable, although the right to transfer them is often more or less restricted."

Advantages

1. Huge amount of capital can be collected from the general public by issue of shares to the general public which is not possible in the case of sole proprietorship and partnership firms.
2. The capital collected by way of shares can be invested in setting up large scale industries, other kind of enterprises or for the expansion of existing enterprises.
3. With the huge capital so raised there can be economies in purchase, management, distribution and selling etc. Thus with enhanced efficiency production will increase and overall cost of production will decrease leading to increase in profits of the company.
4. The liabilities of the shareholders of joint stock company is limited to the face value of shares held by them. Their private properties are not attached to recover the dues of the company. Thus the principle of limited liabilities encourages many investors to invest in the shares of joint stock company.
5. There is restriction on the transfer of shares of the company. Any shareholder can sell or buy the desired number of shares in the stock exchange market. This facility of transfer of shares encourages many persons to invest in the shares of the companies.
6. In a public limited company there is no restriction on the number of members hence a large number of persons can become the members of the company thus a large amount of capital can be collected from the members.
7. A member is free to invest in any number of shares.

8. It stimulates the general public to develop the habit of saving and invest in shares. Thus the public money is utilized for setting up large scale industries and other business enterprises. Ultimately with the establishment of large scale enterprises a large number of persons get employment.
9. In joint stock companies the risk of business loss is divided among the number of shareholders. This encourages the investors to invest their money in shares.
10. The management of the affairs of the company is entrusted to a group of persons known as directors who are elected by the shareholders and they are accountable to the shareholders. In other words it can be said that the ownership of a joint stock company is in the hands of shareholders but the management of the company is in the hands of the board of directors. The shareholders through their voting power decide matters of policy and the directors are to implement this policy. This kind of management is not there in sole proprietorship and partnership organisations.
11. The existence of joint stock company is not affected by the death or bankruptcy of a shareholder. Due to continuity of existence the company can undertake the projects which require long time for their completion.

Disadvantages

1. It is difficult to form a company because so many formalities are required to be completed for its registration with the registrar of companies. All these formalities are time-consuming and expensive as a number of documents are required to be submitted to the registrar of companies.
2. Actually the shareholders are the owners of the company who have invested their hard earned money in the company but they have practically no say in the affairs of the business. The control of the business activities is in the hands of board of directors who are the elected representatives of the shareholders. Sometimes the directors misuse their power and serve their own personal ends ignoring the interest of shareholders.
3. As the directors and managers are salaried persons, sometimes they do not show much interest in the affairs of the company.
4. The shareholders belongs to different far off places scattered throughout the country which makes impossible to conduct the meetings at a short notice to take urgent policy decisions. Thus the business opportunity which must be availed at the appropriate time gets lost due to delay in decision-making.
5. The unscrupulous promoters and directors may misuse the capital collected from the shareholders. Misuse of property, goods and money by the officials of the company may harm the interest of the shareholders and create panic among the public.
6. Sometime bogus companies are floated to cheat the investors of their hard earned money.

7. It is very difficult to wind up a company because a very long and time-consuming procedure has to be followed to wind up a company.

(V) Co-operative Societies

With the industrial revolution the businessmen started exploiting the consumers as well as workers to enrich themselves. This exploitation took the form of long hours of work, lower wages, higher prices and bad service conditions. Economic hardships and other service conditions compelled the workers and other weaker sections of the society to think about mutual help in order to better their economic conditions. This led to the worldwide movement of co-operatives in various fields.

The co-operative movement was started with the basic objective of protecting the economic interests of weaker sections of the society. A co-operative organisation is a voluntary organisations of persons usually with limited means who join together to achieve a common economic end through mutual and self help. Such co-operative organisations registered under Co-operative Societies Act are called "Co-operative Societies".

There are a number of definitions of co-operatives but according to Dr. H.N. Kurzen, "Co-operatives is self help as well as mutual help. It is a joint enterprise of those who are not financially strong and cannot stand on their own legs and therefore come together not with a view to get profits but to overcome disability arising out of the want of adequate financial resources."

The management of the affairs of the society is in the hands of the managing committee which is elected directly by the members of the society. The office bearers of the society include (i) President, (ii) Vice-president, (iii) Secretary, (iv) Joint secretary, (v) Treasurer.

The capital of a co-operative society is collected by its members through purchase of shares. Each member can purchase a limited number of shares as laid down in the rules and regulations of the society. The shares of the society cannot be transferred by a member to another person. However, if a member wants to withdraw his capital he has to return the shares to the society.

Now a days there are a large number of co-operative societies which are working for the upliftment of weaker sections of the society. These societies include :

(a) Co-operative credit societies
(b) Consumer's co-operative stores
(c) Industrial co-operatives or producer's co-operatives
(d) Marketing co-operatives
(e) Co-operative farming societies
(f) Co-operative housing societies

Advantages

1. It is very easy to form co-operative societies. Any ten adult members can voluntarily join together to form the co-operative society. The co-

operative societies so formed can be easily registered with the registrar of societies with simple formalities.

2. The main advantage of co-operative society is to provide service to its members. They provide the quality products at reasonable rates because co-operative societies sell the products at no profit no loss basis. Moreover in the days of scarcity co-operative societies provide the scarce products to its members at reasonable rates.
3. Since the products are made available at reasonable rates to its members so the purchasing power of the members is increased which raises the standard of living of the members. They also help in the removal of social problems like black marketing, profiteering and exploitation etc.
4. The liability of the members of a co-operative society is limited to the face value of the shares held by them.
5. The co-operative societies enjoy the benefit of continuous existence. So the functioning of a society is not affected by the death, insolvency or conviction of a member.
6. Even workers, consumers, farmers and middle class people can become the members of the co-operative societies.
7. Since members of a co-operative society belong to a particular area, particular social or economic group therefore there can be a better co-ordination among themselves leading to healthier, profitable and efficient management activities of the society.
8. In order to boost the co-operative movement the government provides certain benefits to the registered co-operative societies in the form of loans at nominal rate of interest, land at subsidised rates, tax concessions etc. Such concessions are extensively given to co-operative housing societies.

Disadvantages

1. The co-operative societies generally suffer from shortage of capital because the members of these societies mostly belong to the weaker sections of the society.
2. Due to limited resources the co-operative societies may not be in a position to invest in large scale and risky business.
3. There may be differences of opinion among the members of the society which lead to groupism and ultimately the function of the society may be affected.
4. The management of the society is in the hands of the elected members who may not be efficient and experienced to run the affairs of the society effectively.
5. Recurring losses due to inefficiency, misuse of funds, ignorance about rules and regulations of co-operative societies, unnecessary interference by government agencies and political persons may seriously affect the functioning of the co-operative societies.

(B) Public/State Enterprises

Public enterprises are also known as state enterprises. They are owned and controlled by the central government, state government or local government or jointly by these bodies. The public enterprises are financed by the government though in some cases the private investors are also allowed to invest but to a certain extent. The major part of the capital is invested by the government.

Industrial revolution led to the growth of industries in all fields. Mainly the private entrepreneurs set up the industries and started amassing wealth by taking heavy margin of profit. They also started exploiting the workers as well as consumers in order to amass wealth. This led to the setting up of public enterprises so as to provide service to the society i.e. to give employment to maximum number of persons by setting up more and more enterprises, stoppage of exploitation of workers by private enterprises and to provide the goods and services to the public at reasonable prices. Though the public enterprises provide the goods and services to the public at reasonable prices, they also earn a reasonable amount of profit to meet their expenses as well as for future expansion of the enterprises.

Public enterprises invest in those areas where the investments are very high and the chances of earning the profits are not certain or the rate of return is not adequate. Private enterprises do not invest in such areas where the profits are not sure and that too in heavy amounts. So in such areas the government has to invest the public money. Thus public enterprises help in the overall industrialization of the economy specially in the exploitation of natural resources e.g. the Oil and Natural Gas Commission.

The various public enterprises include water, electricity, transport, post and telegraph, banks, Life Insurance Corporation of India, Hindustan Aeronautics Limited, Hindustan Antibiotics, Indian Drugs and Pharmaceuticals Ltd. (IDPL) etc.

REVISION QUESTIONS

(A) Multiple choice questions

Select the right answer and put the correct word in the respective squares given below :

1. The oldest form of business organisation is :
   (a) Partnership (b) Hindu joint family
   (c) Sole proprietorship (d) All the above
2. The maximum number of partners allowed in a general business (non-banking business) is :
   (a) 10 (b) 20
   (c) 50 (d) Unlimited
3. The maximum number of partners allowed in a banking business is :
   (a) 10 (b) 20
   (c) 40 (d) 50

4. The maximum number of members allowed in a public limited company is :
   (a) 10 (b) 20
   (c) 50 (d) Unlimited
5. In which of the following forms of business organisations, registration is compulsory :
   (a) Partnership firm (b) Sole proprietorship firm
   (c) Joint stock company (d) All the above
6. The registration of partnership is :
   (a) Optional
   (b) Compulsory under the Indian Partnership Act, 1932
   (c) Compulsory under the Companies Act, 1956
7. The liability of a partner with regard to the debts of a firm is :
   (a) Limited (b) Unlimited
   (c) No liability
8. A private limited company can start its business :
   (a) On the receipt of certificate of commencement of business
   (b) On the receipt of certificate of incorporation
   (c) On the receipt of both the above mentioned certificates
   (d) None of the above

1	2	3	4	5	6	7	8

(B) Matching type questions

Match the items of Column I with appropriate items in Column II

Column I	Column II
(a) Sole proprietorship business is called	(i) the shareholder can transfer his shares
(b) In joint stock company	(ii) the liability of the partner is limited
(c) In general partnership form	(iii) does not take active part in the business activities
(d) Sleeping partner	(iv) one man business
(e) In co-operative society	(v) is known as firm
(f) Partnership business organisation	(vi) shares of the business cannot be transferred

a	b	c	d	e	f

(C) Very short answer type questions

Define the following :

(i) Business
(ii) Sole proprietorship
(iii) Partnership deed
(iv) Co-operative society
(v) Public company
(vi) Private company
(vii) Joint stock company

(D) Short answer type questions

(a) Differentiate between the following :
   (i) Sole proprietorship and partnership
   (ii) General partnership and limited partnership
   (iii) Limited liability and unlimited liability
   (iv) A firm and a company
   (v) Joint stock company and partnership business organisation

(b) Explain the following :
   (i) Nominal partner
   (ii) Active partner
   (iii) Sleeping partner
   (iv) Minor as a partner
   (v) Partner by estoppel

(c) Describe the salient features of a co-operative society business.

(d) Discuss the main features of a sole proprietorship business organisation.

(E) Long answer type questions

1. What do you understand from the forms of business organisations? Give main characteristics of business organisations.
2. Describe various forms of business organisations on the basis of ownership. Describe sole proprietorship in detail.
3. Write short notes on the following :
   (i) Sole proprietorship business
   (ii) Partnership
   (iii) Joint stock company
   (iv) Co-operative society
   (v) Joint Hindu family firm
   (vi) Public/state enterprises
4. Discuss the advantages and disadvantages of the following types of business organisations :
   (i) Sole proprietorship
   (ii) Partnership firm
   (iii) Joint Hindu family firm
   (iv) Joint stock company
   (v) Co-operative societies
5. What is a partnership firm? Explain different kinds of partnerships.
6. What do you understand from joint stock company? Give its advantages and disadvantages.
7. Explain the characteristic features of co-operatives. Discuss its advantages and disadvantages.

Answers

(A)

1	2	3	4	5	6	7	8
c	b	a	d	c	a	b	b

(B)

a	b	c	d	e	f
(iv)	(i)	(ii)	(iii)	(vi)	(v)

3

Channels of Distribution

The channel of distribution is the last component of the total marketing process. The ultimate aim of every producer is to get the goods delivered to the consumers. He produces various products and after advertisement etc. raises its demand and now the next step is to see that the goods are distributed to the consumers. The path and the link along which goods move from the manufacturer to the consumers is known as channels of distribution. According to William J. Stanton, "A channel of distribution of a product is the route taken by the goods as they move from the producer to ultimate consumer."

Channels of distribution include producers, wholesalers and retailers and sometimes agents are also included. Channels of distribution do not include transport agencies, insurance companies, banks, warehouses and other non-middlemen institutions though they perform very important functions in aid of trade but they do not play any major role in negotiating purchase and sale of products.

Advantages of Channels of Distribution

1. The goods will be available to the consumers all the time at all the places.
2. With the help of channels of distribution the cost in marketing as compared to distribution by the producer himself will be less.
3. With the introduction of channels of distribution more financial sources will come and the financial burden on the producer will be decreased.
4. Since more persons are involved in the distribution of same goods so each will try to advertise the same product which will increase the sales.
5. It helps in reasonable price fixation since many persons are involved and monopoly is broken.
6. It gives more employment opportunities which ultimately increases standard of living.
7. It solves the distribution problems of the producers. He will distribute the goods to the wholesalers or retailers and not to the customers.

Factors to be taken into consideration in the selection of channels of distribution

Channels of distribution are the most powerful elements for the sale of products. Though the products may be of very high quality but they will lose their importance if they do not find the right path of distribution. On the other hand, by developing a sound channel of distribution even low grade products can be sold without facing much difficulties. Hence while selecting the channels of distribution the following factors must be taken into consideration by the manufa

1. Nature of Goods

The manufacturer will have to see the type of goods before deciding the channels of distribution. The products intended for industrial use like heavy machinery, raw materials in bulk quantities or costly items are supplied direct to the consumer industries.

The standardised and brand named goods can be sold directly through manufacturer's own sales organisations but if the goods are new he will have to take the help of wholesalers and retailers.

For perishable goods a channel will have to be selected which will deliver the goods to the consumers at the earliest.

If a manufacturer manufactures only one type of product, he can sell it directly to the consumers but if he manufactures different kinds of items then he will have to appoint wholesalers and retailers because in this way he will be able to deliver the goods to a large number of customers.

2. Nature and Extent of Market

The study of the market will show the number, location and buying habits of the consumers and accordingly the manufacturer will have to choose the channel.

3. Review of Existing Channels

In different industries there are well established different methods of distribution which have been accepted by the customers therefore he will have to choose a channel on existing lines.

4. Customer Buying Habits

The buying habits of customers also play a major role in the selection of channel of distribution. If the customers want to buy goods from wide range of varieties and at certain times when he is willing to spend then the manufacturer will have to appoint the wholesalers and retailers so as to provide wide variety of goods to the customers.

5. Mutual Co-operation between the Manufacturers and Middle Men

Mutual co-operation and assistance received from the wholesalers and retailers is also an important factor in deciding the channel. Sometimes middlemen are not prepared to sell the products of a particular manufacturer because the policies may not suit to the middlemen. For example the middleman is interested that he should be the sole selling agent for a particular area or he wants to get the goods on credit for a longer period whereas the manufacturer is not prepared to agree to these points. So under such circumstances he will have to decide which channel of distribution will be most suitable.

Different Channels of Distribution

Different channels of distribution can be grouped into two main groups as given below :

A. Direct selling

B. Indirect selling

A. Direct Selling

In direct selling the manufacturers sell their products direct to the ultimate consumers by employing their own salesmen or middlemen who visit the consumers. Now a days direct selling is gaining popularity and many manufacturers are adopting this method for selling their products. Goods which are sold in this way include cosmetics, household goods etc. Eureka Forbes Ltd. (EFL) a Bombay based company which markets vacuum cleaners is sending their salesmen from door to door who give live demonstration and canvass the ultimate consumers to buy their products.

Advantages

Direct selling has the advantages that :

(a) The middlemen are eliminated.

(b) The consumer is given all kinds of information regarding the product on the spot.

(c) The consumer is directly given the incentives.

(d) The manufacturer can collect immediate feedback information.

MIDDLEMEN

Middlemen are the persons who act as link between the producer and the consumer. They are primarily engaged in marketing and help in purchase and sale of goods and services. Thus they constitute an important link in the channel of distribution. Middlemen specialize in different fields of business hence render good services to manufacturers and ultimate consumers. They charge for their services rendered to manufacturers and consumers.

Middlemen help the manufacturers in the sale of products because in the absence of these middlemen they will have to perform all the functions involved in the sale of products themselves. Middlemen are helpful to the consumers in getting their demands satisfied regarding particular products.

Types of Middlemen

Middlemen are broadly classified into two categories :

(i) Merchantile agents

(ii) Merchant middlemen.

(i) Merchantile Agents

Merchantile agents are also known as 'functional middlemen' or 'agent middlemen'. They are those intermediaries who perform various marketing functions without having any title to goods. They act on behalf of others in arranging the goods and pass on the same to the users. In this matter they themselves do not invest anything but they get their share for the services rendered by them. Merchantile agents are of the following types :

(a) Brokers
(b) Commission agents
(c) Auctioneers

(a) Brokers

Brokers are those agents who bring the buyers and sellers together and negotiate purchase and sale of goods on behalf of buyers and sellers, the terms of which are acceptable to both the parties. They are called selling agent if they are engaged by the seller and buying agent if they are engaged by the buyer for the negotiation of terms. They neither get the possession nor acquire ownership of the goods. They simply get certain percentage of commission (known as brokerage) on the business transacted by them.

(b) Commission Agents

Commission agents also sell goods on behalf of the seller but they differ from brokers that they not only negotiate the sale of goods but also take possession of the goods and make arrangements for the transfer of title to the goods. They make necessary arrangements for warehousing, grading, packing, assembling and dispersion of goods. If need arises they lend money in advance to the sellers. A commission agent may also be employed for the purchase of goods on behalf of the purchaser. For their services the commission agents get a certain percentage of commission on sales.

(c) Auctioneers

Auctioneers are the merchantile agents who sell goods on behalf of their principals by undertaking auction of goods. The auctioneers take possession of goods from the sellers, displays them before the intending buyers and receives bid from the purchasers (bid means the price which the buyer is willing to pay for the goods being auctioned). The bidder who gives the highest bid gets the goods provided the highest bid is at least equal to the minimum reserve price fixed for the purpose. If the highest bid happens to be lower than the minimum reserve price fixed then the auctioneer can cancel the auction. An auctioneer receives a certain percentage of commission on sale proceeds of goods for the services rendered by him.

(ii) Merchant Middlemen

Merchant middlemen are the merchants who purchase the goods to resell them for a margin of profit. They take possession and become owner of the products and transfer title of ownership to the buyer when the goods are sold. The merchant middlemen may be classified as follows :

(a) Wholesaler
(b) Retailer

B. Indirect Selling

The indirect selling is done through :

(a) Wholesale trade
(b) Retail Trade

WHOLESALE TRADE

Wholesale trade means buying and selling the goods in large quantities and generally deal in a narrow range of goods which are purchased in large quantities from the producers and are sold in not so large quantities to retailers for resale or to industrial users directly but very rarely to the ultimate consumers. The persons dealing in wholesale business are known as wholesalers. The wholesalers are described as connecting links between the manufacturers and retailers.

Types of Wholesalers

1. Manufacturer Wholesalers

They manufacture the goods and sell them in wholesale. At the same time they also purchase the goods of other manufacturers and sell them along with their own products. In this way their turnover is increased and sale price and overhead expenses are reduced by eliminating the wholesalers.

2. Retailer Wholesalers

They purchase the goods in large quantities directly from the producers and sell them both to the retailers as well as to the consumers.

3. Pure Wholesalers

They deal only in wholesale business. They neither manufacture nor sell the goods direct to the consumers. They purchase the goods in bulk from the manufacturers and sell them in small lots to retailers. Sometimes they engage their own vehicles to distribute the goods to retailers. They may be either mill supply wholesaler, single product wholesaler or multiproducts wholesaler.

A wholesaler may work on commission basis or on regular income basis. A wholesaler may be appointed according to the area covered i.e. local, district level, division level or state level.

Functions of Wholesalers

1. Assembly of Goods

He places orders to various producers and collects different types of goods at one place and resells them to the retailers.

2. Distribution

The wholesalers help in the distribution of goods to the consumers through the retailers.

3. Storage

The wholesalers store the goods for both the producers and retailers. The storage of goods is needed on account of time gap between production and consumption of goods. The goods are also stored to meet the demands of the retailers.

4. Financing

The wholesalers generally advance money to the producers and sell goods on credit to the retailers thus financing both of them.

5. Grading and Packing

Sometimes the wholesalers also undertake the work of grading the goods according to their quality and packing them in different containers before supplying to the retailers.

6. Transportation

The wholesalers purchase the goods in large quantities and supply them in small lots to the retailers who are widely scattered at far off places. For this purpose they may employ their own vehicles or hired vehicles. In this way the botheration of retailers for transportation of goods will be saved. He will receive the goods at his retail outlet.

7. Risk Bearing

The wholesalers bear a lot of risk by bulk purchasing and storing because the goods can become outdated, the price may go down or non-recovery of payment from retailers or there can be damage due to theft, fire etc.

8. Providing Market Information

The wholesalers provide valuable information to both the manufacturers and retailers. He collects the information by market survey and passes it on to the manufacturers regarding the tastes, preferences, likes and dislikes of the customers. Similarly he keeps informing the retailers about the price fluctuation and new products of the manufacturers.

Advantages of Wholesale Trade

A. To producers :

- (i) Helps in large scale production by giving advance orders.
- (ii) Feedback information regarding market.
- (iii) Helps in marketing functions like advertisement.
- (iv) Shares risk of the producer by bulk buying and storage.
- (v) It renders financial help by giving advance.
- (vi) They help in adjusting demand and supply thus help in stabilizing the price of goods.

B. To retailers :

- (i) He collects goods from various producers for resale to retailers.
- (ii) He sells the goods in small quantities to the retailers which the producer might not have given directly to the retailers.

(iii) He provides credit facilities to the retailers thus helps him financially.
(iv) He helps in making the retailer free from the risk of large stock.
(v) He informs the retailer regarding fluctuation in prices and about the new products of the manufacturers.
(vi) He gives trade discount on bulk purchasing by the retailers.
(vii) He undertake large scale advertisement for the products by which the retailers are benefited and their sales are enhanced.
(viii) Generally the wholesalers supply the goods at the business places of the retailers by employing their own vehicles or hired vehicles.

C. Services to consumers and society :

(i) He provides an opportunity to the consumer to select the best of various products in accordance with his tastes, fashions and demand which he has supplied to the retailers.
(ii) He provides latest information of the products by advertising.
(iii) He helps in keeping the prices in control by constantly supplying enough goods.
(iv) He stores sufficient quantities of goods thus minimises the probability of scarcity of goods in the market.

Disadvantages of Wholesalers

(i) They increase the price of goods by increasing their margin of profit.
(ii) They create artificial scarcity by hoarding.
(iii) Sometimes they supply duplicate goods.
(iv) No proper services are rendered as compared to their margin of profit.

(b) Retail Trade

Retailing is the final stage in distribution of goods and involves direct selling to the ultimate consumers. The persons who deal in retail sale of goods are known as retailers. A retailer is a direct link between manufacturer and/or wholesaler and consumer.

Functions of Retailing

(i) Assembling of Goods

Retailers collect variety of goods from different wholesalers to satisfy the demands of the consumers.

(ii) Transportation

Retailers bring the goods from the wholesalers to their shops and then provide free home delivery to their customers.

(iii) Storage

They store goods till they are demanded by the customers. The goods are kept as reserve stocks in order to ensure uninterrupted supply to the consumers.

(iv) Credit Facility

They grant credit facility to their regular customers.

(v) Risk Bearing

The retailers bear the risk of bad debits on account of non-payment of purchases made by the customers. He bears other risks like fire, theft, spoilage, date of expiry risk and change in demand risk etc.

(vi) Market Research

Because of their contact with the consumers they are in a better position to gauge (judge) the tastes and needs of the customers which can be passed on to the producer through the wholesalers for remedial actions.

Advantages

A. Advantages to manufacturers and wholesalers :

(i) They are the last link between the producer and the customer and help in the distribution of goods.

(ii) They take over the function of dealing with large number of persons and selling goods in very small quantities thus relieve the wholesalers from this job.

(iii) Without the services of the retailers it is not possible to introduce a new product in the market.

(iv) They provide the latest information with regard to tastes, fashions and demand of the consumers to the wholesalers who in turn transmit the same to the producers.

(v) Sometimes they make advance payments for the goods to be received thus help in financing the wholesalers.

B. Services to consumers :

(i) They sell goods to the consumers in the smallest possible quantities according to the needs of the customers.

(ii) They keep large variety of goods and thus offer a wide choice to the customers.

(iii) The retailer keeps personal contacts with the customers, listens to their complaints and tries to satisfy them. He passes these genuine complaints to the manufacturers/wholesalers for rectification or substitution of goods.

(iv) They advice the customers regarding the suitability, use and maintenance of the products.

(v) They also provide free home delivery and after sales services to regular customers.

(vi) The retailers often grant credit facility to the needy customers thereby helping them in times of difficulty.

(vii) They allow cash discount to the consumers on the products sold.

(viii) They provide fresh and latest products to the customers.

(ix) Since the retail shops are generally situated near the residential areas so it is convenient for the customers to meet their daily requirements.

(x) Some of the retailers render day and night services which is very helpful in emergency cases.

Types of Retailers

A Itinerant retailers :
Peddlers, hawkers and street traders.

B. Fixed shop small scale retailers :
(i) Street stall holders
(ii) Second hand good retailers
(iii) General shops
(iv) Speciality shops

C. Fixed shop large scale retailers :
(i) Departmental stores
(ii) Multiple shops
(iii) Mail order business
(iv) Super markets
(v) Co-operative stores
(vi) Hire-purchase shops.

I. Itinerant Retailers

These retailers do not have any fixed place or shop to carry on their business. They generally move from one place to another to sell their goods. They carry the goods on their heads or on some kind of vehicles. They need very limited money to carry on their business. They generally deal in those articles which can be sold easily during the day e.g. vegetables, fruits, milk and other eatable articles. Such retailers can be seen along the road sides, streets, bus stands, railway compartments, fairs etc.

2. Departmental Stores

A departmental store is a big store engaged in the retail trade of wide variety of goods under the same roof. There may be separate departments for clothes, readymade garments, books, medicines, groceries etc., however the management is the same.

Advantages of Departmental Stores

(i) Since a departmental store purchases goods in large quantities thereby it can avail economies of large scale buying, transportation costs and trade discount etc.

(ii) Customers do not have to run from one shop to another. Here they can practically buy everything at the same place.

(iii) Departmental stores can make extensive use of advertisement.

(iv) Some of the departmental stores provide various services to customers such as free home delivery, after sales services, accepting orders on telephones and credit facilities.

(v) Some of the departmental stores provide recreational facilities, bank, telephone, post and telegraph services etc.

(vi) They can hire professionals and experts.

(vii) Due to large volume of sales and large turnover, the overall selling costs per unit are reduced.

Disadvantages of departmental stores

(i) The initial cost of running the business is very high.

(ii) Since the departmental stores provide various specialized services to customers and undertake extensive advertising which leads to higher overhead charges and operational costs.

(iii) Due to high operational costs the prices of goods charged from the customers are comparatively higher.

(iv) Generally departmental stores are located at central places of the city therefore people living at distant places cannot visit these stores easily.

(v) Since there are too many sections and large number of employees work in a departmental store, it is very difficult for the owner of the store to establish proper co-ordination and supervision of their functioning.

(vi) Due to big rush the personal contacts between the owner of store and customers may not be established which may affect the sales. Some of the salesmen may not attend the customers properly and satisfy their demands.

3. Multiple Shops or Chain Stores

Multiple shops consist of a chain of stores in a city, throughout the state/country and are organised by a centralised agency for selling the same kind of products. As multiple shops are owned and managed by a central organisation, the uniformity of operations is the basic feature of this form of retailing. Examples of multiple shops are Bata, D.C.M., Usha appliances etc.

Characteristics of multiple shops

(i) Multiple shops specialize in one or a few types of goods.

(ii) When organised by manufacturers, multiple shops aim at eliminating both wholesalers and retailers.

(iii) Purchasing, assembling, transporting, advertising and financing etc. for all the multiple shops are made by the central office.

(iv) Generally the multiple shops have the same design, decoration and layout.

(v) The prices charged for the goods are fixed and are the same every where.

(vi) They generally sell goods on cash and carry basis and do not allow credit and free delivery services to customers.

(vii) They generally deal in consumer goods.

Advantages of multiple shops

(i) The prices are fixed and no bargaining is done.
(ii) Generally quality goods are sold.
(iii) Due to lower operational costs the prices of goods are generally lower.
(iv) Common advertisement is done from a centralised place which covers the entire national network.
(v) Since they work on cash and carry principle so the chances of bad debt are minimum.
(vi) Better market research can be done because of direct contact with the consumers.
(vii) The problem of dead stock is almost eliminated because if certain product is not sold on one shop the same may be transferred to another shop where these items can be sold out.
(viii) Multiple shops can be easily identified because of uniform pattern of design and decoration of the shops.

Disadvantages of multiple shops

(i) These shops do not give any credit facility to the customers which has a negative effect on sales.
(ii) They do not provide any home delivery service to the consumers.
(iii) Since only the staff employed runs the shops they may not give full attention towards customers satisfaction as well as they may not be faithful to the owner.
(iv) To run chain stores heavy investments and faithful persons are required to look after the business.
(v) Customer's choice is limited since chain stores deal only in limited range of products.

4. Mail Order Business

A mail order business is a kind of retail trade where business is carried on through post. The orders are received by post and goods are sent to the customers by post.

Under this system of retailing a contact is established with the customers through advertisements like press, radio, T.V., sending price lists, samples, circulars or leaflets etc. giving details of the product. Sometimes the mail order houses send reply paid postage cards to the prospective buyers. In this case the buyer does not meet the seller or vice versa. After satisfying himself, the customer places the order for the goods by post. The goods are then dispatched to the customers usually through V.P.P. (value payable parcel) or by registered post. Sometimes goods are also sent by railways or transport agencies. The railways or transport bilties are sent to respective banks and the customers are informed accordingly. After paying the amount to the bank the bilti is released. After presenting the bilti to the delivery office of railways or transport agencies the goods are handed over to the customers. In the case of goods sent by V.P.P. the postman brings the parcel to the customer, after collecting the said money he hands over the parcel to the customer. The money so collected is sent back to the mail order houses by means of V.P.P. order forms (similar to that of money order forms). So the whole process is carried on by post therefore the mail order business is also described as "shopping by post".

Characteristics of mail order business

(i) There is no need of large capital.
(ii) There is no need of middlemen.
(iii) There is no need of keeping the goods in godowns. Moreover no shop is required because business can be carried on from house itself.
(iv) It is purely based on advertisements.
(v) The orders are placed by post only.
(vi) The goods are generally dispatched by V.P.P. or by registered post.

Advantages of mail order business

1. The buyer is not required to travel to get the delivery of goods. He will get them at his residence by means of V.P.P.
2. The buyer is generally given a money back guarantee.
3. Since the overhead expenses of the mail order houses like show room rent, salesmen's salaries, commission to middlemen etc. are not required therefore it is an economical operation.
4. Since the goods are sent by V.P.P. the chances of bad debt are negligible.
5. It is very useful for those buyers who are sitting at far off and remote places.
6. There is no need of large investment in the business.
7. There is no need of storing the goods. The same may be procured as and when the order is received.
8. There is no need of appointing the middlemen.

Disadvantages

1. There is lack of personal contact and hence buyer cannot inspect the goods before purchasing.
2. Goods sent by post are costlier because postal expenses are also to be met by the customer.
3. Sometimes postal delay may cause inconvenience to the buyer.
4. Fraud can be done on innocent customers.
5. No after sales services can be rendered to the customers.
6. The customers are deprived of credit facilities.
7. This system is not suitable for all types of goods. It can be used only for a specific type of goods.
8. This system is suitable only to the educated persons.
9. Lot of money is spent on advertisements.
10. Mail order business is not suitable for bulky and perishable goods.
11. In mail order business there is risk of loss of goods during transit.

5. Super Markets

Super markets are also known as 'Super Bazars'. They are large scale retail institutions having different departments which work under one roof. These bazars deal mainly in food articles, grocery items, cloth and medicines etc. The main feature of these markets is that they do not employ salesmen and shop assistants to help the customers. The customer himself picks up his requirements from different racks in a bucket which are then brought for payment to the cashier who sits near the exit door. After making the payment the customer is allowed to take the goods. Due to this reason these markets are also known as 'self service stores'. These markets operate strictly on cash and carry principle and do not provide any credit and after sales services facilities to the customers.

These types of stores are very popular in U.S.A. and other foreign countries. In India these Super Bazars exist only in big cities and only a few have the self service facilities whereas at others salesmen meet the demands of the customers.

6. Consumers Co-operative Stores

In this system the consumers themselves form a society which runs the store. The main purpose of such stores is to eliminate the middlemen. The goods are purchased in bulk direct from the manufacturers/wholesalers and are sold to the customers in small quantities at market rates. A part of the profit thus earned is distributed among the members of the society in the form of bonus.

Advantages

1. The overall cost of the products is reduced since they are purchased in bulk direct from the manufacturers. Thus the middleman's profit is eliminated.
2. The consumers get good quality products since the chances of adulteration are not there which is generally practised by some retailers in the private sector.
3. Consumers are assured of availability of certain products even when there is an overall shortage of those products in the market and that too at reasonable rates.
4. The overhead expenses are reduced since unnecessary expenditure on advertisement and decoration of store is not required. The expenditure due to wages of employees is also reduced since less number of employees can serve the purpose.

Disadvantages

1. The societies have very limited resources so these stores cannot run on large scale.
2. The people in general do not visit such stores regularly. They come to buy the things when there is scarcity of the products in the market.
3. All the members of the society may not be co-operative and responsible hence these stores tend to suffer financial losses.

7. Hire Purchase System

In this system the purchaser gets the immediate possession of the goods without paying the full amount to the seller. A part of payment is made at the time of purchase and the balance is paid in easy instalments spread over a specified period. In this system the buyer becomes the owner of goods only after paying the full amount to the seller. If a purchaser does not pay the instalment(s) the seller is free to carry back the goods. The whole system works on an agreement signed between the sellers and the buyer with or without guarantors (sureties).

Advantages

(i) Hire purchase system is usually carried on in case of durable costly consumer articles like radios, televisions, refrigerators, cycles, scooters etc.
(ii) This system is quite useful for people having limited income because they can pay the amount in easy instalments.
(iii) This system helps to increase the sale of costly items because it tempts a large number of people to buy the same.
(iv) Even the people who have enough money to buy are tempted to buy on hire purchase system because the money for the item is to be paid in easy instalments and they can invest their own money elsewhere.
(v) This system is very helpful to salaried class of people.

Disadvantages

(i) The people are tempted by the instalment schemes to buy the products which they are unable to afford.
(ii) The buyer has to pay a higher price which includes the cost and interest on unpaid instalments.
(iii) Some of the buyers become defaulters because they are unable to pay heavy instalments.
(iv) The traders dealing in hire purchase system have to arrange a large capital to run the business.

Channels of distribution for pharmaceuticals/drugs

The pharmaceuticals/drugs can't be distributed or sold direct to the consumers which is the major difference between the sale of drugs and ordinary consumable goods. They will have to be recommended by a physician or a doctor and dispensed by a registered pharmacist. Moreover a licence is required for the sale of drugs.

Generally the following channels are selected for the distribution of drugs from manufacturer to consumer :

Manufacturer → Wholesaler → Retailer → Consumer

(a) Wholesale
(b) Retail sale

(a) Wholesale

Basically the wholesale of drugs and pharmaceuticals is quite similar to the wholesale trade of other consumable goods as discussed earlier in detail but differs in the following respects :

(i) A drug licence is required for the wholesale business of drugs.
(ii) Only a qualified person according to Drugs and Cosmetics Act, 1948 is authorised to do wholesale business of drugs.
(iii) A wholesaler cannot sell the drugs direct to the consumers.

Manufacturers generally appoint stockists, distributors or wholesalers for the sale of drugs. They supply the drugs to these stockists or wholesalers who further supply the drugs to hospitals, research institutions, practising practitioners and retailers. The retailers sell the drugs to consumers or patients. The sale of drugs by the stockists or wholesalers to the retailers is known as wholesale trade and the sale of drugs by the retailers to the consumers or patients is known as retail trade.

The following conditions are necessary for the grant of licence for wholesale of drugs :

(i) The licencee must have adequate premises not less than 10 square meters in area which should have facilities for the storage as well as to maintain the potency of drugs.
(ii) The licencee must be a qualified person according to the Act.
(iii) He will stock only those categories of drugs for which licence is granted i.e. whether the licence is granted for the sale of Schedule C and C_1 drugs or other than Schedule C and C_1 drugs or both.
(iv) He will be permitted to sell the drugs only from the premises for which licence is granted.
(v) He will maintain the proper record of purchase and sale of drugs.
(vi) He will display the licence at a prominent place of the premises open to the public.
(vii) If there is any change in the qualified staff he will immediately inform about the same to the licensing authority.

(b) Retail Sale

Basically the retail sale of drugs is similar to general consumable goods already discussed in detail but it differs in the following respects :

(i) A drug licence is required for the retail sale of drugs.
(ii) A qualified person i.e. qualified pharmacist is authorised to sell the drugs.
(iii) Most of the drugs are sold to consumers only on presentation of prescription from the physician.
(iv) A physician is the only decision maker regarding the selection of a drug. The selection is not in the hands of a retailer or a consumer while the sale of ordinary goods is an open trade where the consumer is at liberty to select the goods of his own choice.
(v) Home delivery of drugs is not made.

The following conditions are necessary for the grant of licence for retail sale of drugs :

(i) The licencee must have adequate premises which should have sufficient facilities for the storage as well as to maintain the potency of drugs.

(ii) The licencee must be a qualified pharmacist.

(iii) The licencee will stock only those categories of drugs for which licence is granted i.e. whether the licence is granted for the sale of Schedule C and C_1 drugs or other than Schedule C and C_1 drugs or both.

(iv) He will be permitted to sell the drugs only from the premises for which licence is granted.

(v) He will maintain the proper record of purchase and sale of drugs.

(vi) He will display the licence at a prominent place of the premises open to the public.

(vii) If there is any change in the qualified staff he will immediately inform about the same to the licensing authority.

(viii) Licencee must allow an authorised inspector to inspect the premises, registers and records to verify whether the provision of the Act and Rules are being observed.

Retail Vending of Drugs

Under certain circumstances drugs are allowed to be sold by vendors who have no fixed place of business but move from one place to another to meet the demands of customers. They are granted licences by the licensing authority for the retail sale of drugs in a particular area. Such licences are issued to the persons who undertake the distribution of drugs in sparsely populated areas or far-flung areas where there are no other agencies for the distribution of drugs. The persons who are granted such licences are permitted to sell drugs other than those specified in Schedule C and C_1. The licences of such persons can be cancelled if they violate the rules of the act.

Functions of Retailers

A chemist has to perform the following functions :

(i) Estimation

Retailers estimate the probable demand by the physicians through the consumers for various types of drugs prescribed by him.

(ii) Assembling the Drugs

Retailers collect variety of drugs from different wholesalers to satisfy the demand of the consumers.

(iii) Transportation

Retailers bring the drugs from the wholesalers to their shops.

(iv) Storage

They store the drugs till they are demanded by the consumers. The drugs are kept as reserve stocks in order to ensure uninterrupted supply to consumers.

(v) Customer Services

Some of the retailers render day and night services which is very helpful in emergency cases.

(vi) Market Research

Since the retailer is in direct contact with the consumers so they are very important source of information regarding the prescribing trends of doctors around him. He can give the information regarding the movement of drugs of other competitive manufacturers. The information so collected may be passed on to wholesalers who will ultimately supply this information to manufacturers.

REVISION QUESTIONS

(A) Multiple choice questions

Select the right answer and put the correct word in the respective squares given below :

1. A retailer is in direct link with :
   (a) Consumer (b) Wholesaler
   (c) Manufacturer (d) Both (a) and (b)
   (e) Both (b) and (c)
2. A wholesaler acts as a link between :
   (a) Retailer (b) Manufacturer
   (c) Both (a) and (b) (d) None of the above
3. Wholesalers should be removed from the channels of distribution because :
   (a) They act as link between retailers and producers
   (b) They collect different varieties of goods at one place
   (c) They help in increasing the production
   (d) They increase the price of goods
4. Heavy machinery is sold to the consumer by :
   (a) Direct selling (b) Indirect selling
   (c) Functional middlemen (d) Merchant middlemen
5. Mail order business is :
   (a) Retail trade (b) Wholesale trade
   (c) Retail trade by post (d) None of the above
6. In mail order business goods are sold :
   (a) On credit basis (b) On instalment basis
   (c) On cash basis (d) Both cash and credit basis
7. Itinerant retailers sell the goods from :
   (a) Fixed premises (b) Moving from place to place
   (c) Street stalls (d) None of the above
8. Multiple shops deals in :
   (a) Same type of goods (b) All types of goods

(c) Different types of goods according to their own choice
(d) Specified same type of goods

1	2	3	4	5	6	7	8

(B) Matching type questions

Match the items of Column I with appropriate items in Column II.

Column I	Column II
(a) A retailer who sells goods by moving from one place to another	(i) Retailer and manufacturer
(b) A retailer who deals in drugs	(ii) Consumer and wholesaler
(c) A retail trade done by post only	(iii) Itinerant retailers
(d) A retailer is a link between	(iv) Chemist
(e) A wholesaler is a link between	(v) Mail order business

a	b	c	d	e

(C) Very short-answer type questions

Define the following terms :

(i) Channel of distribution
(ii) Retailer
(iii) Wholesaler
(iv) Broker
(v) Commission agent
(vi) Multiple shops
(vii) Consumer co-operative store

(D) Short-answer type questions

1. What do you understand from the term channels of distribution? Discuss advantages of channels of distribution.
2. Describe the advantages and disadvantages of retailers.
3. Discuss the functions of a wholesaler.
4. Describe in brief what you know about the merchant middlemen.
5. Write in brief about multiple shops.
6. Discuss the salient features of a departmental store.
7. Explain the main features of a mail order business.

(E) Long-answer type questions

1. What do you understand from the term channels of distribution? Describe various advantages of channels of distribution. Explain different factors to be taken into consideration in the selection of channels of distribution.

2. Define the term middlemen. Enumerate briefly various types of middlemen and explain merchantile agents in detail.
3. Write short notes on the following :
   (i) Retailer (ii) Wholesaler
   (iii) Middlemen (iv) Brokers
   (v) Commission agents (vi) Auctioneers
   (vii) Mail order business (viii) Multiple shops
   (ix) Departmental stores (x) Co-operative stores
   (xi) Types of retailers
4. Define the term wholesaler. Describe various functions, advantages and disadvantages of wholesalers.
5. Who is a retailer? Describe various functions and advantages of retailing.
6. What do you understand from the term retailer? Explain various types of retailers.
7. Explain the following :
   (a) Advantages and disadvantages of departmental stores.
   (b) Characteristics of multiple stores.
   (c) Advantages and disadvantages of multiple stores.
8. What do you mean by "Mail order business"? Explain the characteristic features, advantages and disadvantages of mail order business.
9. Write short notes on the following :
   (a) Supermarkets (b) Hire purchase system
   (c) Itinerant retailers
10. Differentiate between the following :
    (a) Retail trade and wholesale trade
    (b) Departmental store and multiple shops
    (c) Mail order business and hire purchase system
11. Explain various channels of distribution for pharmaceuticals/drugs. Discuss what are the conditions required for the grant of licence for wholesale of drugs.
12. Describe how the retailsale of ordinary goods differs from retailsale of drugs. Discuss the conditions required for the grant of licence for retailsale of drugs.

Answers

(A)

1	2	3	4	5	6	7	8
d	c	d	a	c	c	b	d

(B)

a	b	c	d	e
(iii)	(iv)	(v)	(ii)	(i)

4

Drug House Management

After attaining the required qualification in Pharmacy i.e. Diploma in Pharmacy (D.Pharm) or Bachelor in Pharmacy (B.Pharm) and prescribed experience, there are a number of avenues open for a pharmacist. Due to his training in many scientific disciplines he can work effectively and efficiently in various fields of pharmacy such as community pharmacy, hospital pharmacy, retail pharmacy, wholesale pharmacy, pharmaceutical education, drug manufacturing houses as helpers of manufacturing chemists, analysts, supervisors or they may work as medical detailmen. The most effective use of a pharmacist is to train him as a medical detailman because he is the only person educated as an expert on drugs. They may also serve in the Army, Navy and Air Force. Pharmacist may get employment in banks, various financial institutions, teaching institutions, Food and Drug Administration, and various other areas.

The pharmacist who has an aptitude for business, financially sound and ready to invest money in business can open a retailsale/wholesale drug store. The success of a drug store depends on a number of factors some of which are given below :

(i) Its location and proper layout design.
(ii) Sound financial management.
(iii) Qualified and experienced staff.
(iv) Honesty, sincerity and hard work.
(v) Behaviour among staff members and with customers.

Whenever a person decides to open a drug store the most important consideration before him is the selection of a suitable site because for the success of any business, selection of site is of prime importance.

Factors for the selection of site of a retailsale drug store

For the selection of site of a retailsale drug store following factors must be taken into consideration :

(i) Availability of Finance

Availability of finance is the most important factor for the selection of site. If the person is having sufficient finances he can open the drug store in an urban and well developed area but if he is having meager financial resources then he can open a drug store in a village, small town or newly developing area on the outskirts of urban area.

(ii) Density of population

Thickly populated area may be preferred than the area with less population because the demand of medicines in thickly populated area will be more.

(iii) Buying habits of the public

Sale of medicines depends on the buying habits and buying capacity of the public. Rich people can afford to buy the costly medicines who live in less populated area but on the other hand poor people may not be in a position to purchase the medicines who are living in thickly populated area.

(iv) Number of doctors in the surrounding area

That area will be most suitable for opening a drug store where two or three physicians are doing practice and their practice is quite good. It is the general trend that the physicians prescribe the medicines to the patients and charge the consultation fee only. The patients are asked to purchase the medicines from the market. So the patient will try to buy the medicines from the nearby chemist shop. But if they are dispensing physicians (i.e. selling own medicines) then they will prove to be competitors for the drug store.

(v) Existence of hospital

The site near the hospital or the dispensary is most suitable for opening a drug store provided that (a) hospital does not maintain its own drug store, (b) the doctors write good number of prescriptions to the outdoor and indoor patients.

Nowadays a number of private nursing homes and hospitals are being opened in rural as well as urban areas. Generally these types of nursing homes and hospitals have their own drug stores but even then a drug store can be opened where two or more such nursing homes are existing.

(vi) Number of drug stores existing in the area

That area should be selected where no other chemist shop exists. But if the potential is very high and already a number of chemist shops are existing then this area may be selected because this area may become a major business centre of drugs as the people generally think that all types of drugs are available from this area because of existence of large number of drug stores. With this idea in mind, a large number of people will visit the area and in turn sales will enhance.

(vii) Business locality

Since a large number of people visit the shopping centres daily for meeting their requirements, so a drug store can be opened in the shopping centre. When the customers buy the other products, they may also purchase the medicines. However, the main hindrance in opening a drug store in such a locality is that :

(a) Shop is not easily available.
(b) Land price is very high.
(c) Huge investment is required to maintain the standard of the drug store.

(viii) Flow of traffic

A drug store should not be opened near the traffic signals as well as road circles because of parking problems and traffic jams. It should be opened on that side of the road which takes people to their homes because people prefer to buy the goods while returning from their place of work.

Drug store in rural area or small town

When a pharmacist is not in a position to invest huge amount for opening a drug store in an urban area he can open the drug store in rural area or a small town. In the rural area he can get loan from nationalised and co-operative banks at a very nominal rate of interest and easy terms and conditions. These banks also provide various kinds of incentives for purchasing the inventories for the drug store.

In the rural area the site of drug store should be :

(a) In the main market where large number of people go for shopping.
(b) Near the bus stand or railway station.
(c) Near the village dispensary.
(d) Near the clinics of private practitioners.

Apart from above mentioned points the purchasing power, buying habits, habitation of the people living over there must also be taken into consideration.

Space layout or layout design of a drug store

After selecting the proper site for the location of the drug store the next important step is the space layout or layout design of the drug store. Layout design is concerned with the internal set up and arrangement of the store in a proper manner. Layout design is an art and technique of setting up of the store which everybody can't do it. So it is a fundamental problem faced by all types of organisations specially the retail stores. Therefore technical persons are engaged in setting up the layout design of the retail stores.

Objectives of layout design

(i) To provide attractive look and professional image to the customers.
(ii) To attract more and more customers.
(iii) To increase the sale of the store which is the overall objective.
(iv) To have the best utilisation of the available space.

(v) To provide maximum storage facilities.

(vi) To provide space for reserve stock, office and resting place for the employees.

(vii) To control movement of customers inside the store.

(viii) To protect the medicines from any kind of damage and to maintain their potency.

(ix) To provide surveillance so as to reduce chances of pilferage and theft.

The aim of any drug store is to earn maximum profit which is only possible if a large number of customers visit the store and do the purchasing. For this purpose the layout design of the drug store is prepared in such a way which reduces the cost and increases the profits. The possibilities of future expansion of the business and alterations to be made in layout design should also be taken into consideration.

The drug store should be constructed with cement and concrete and marble or mosaic tiles fitted on the floor. Preferably the walls and roof should be painted with washable paint for easy cleaning. The wooden or steel racks should be painted white from inside and fitted with glass doors. The counters should be made from wood having white sunmica at the top. The show windows should be made very attractive and tastefully decorated. Office furniture such as table and sufficient number of chairs should be provided. There should be sufficient waiting space with comfortable chairs for the customers. Sufficient lighting (fluorescent tubes) should be provided which helps in quick identification of goods and gives cheerful atmosphere to the customers and staff working over there. If possible, toilet facilities should be provided inside the store for use by the staff.

The layout design of an ideal retail drug store is given on the following page.

All the medicines and accessories must be put on the shelves. The fast moving items must be kept handy near the counter. The slow moving drugs or the drugs which are not used frequently may be kept on the upper shelves. The bulky items should be kept on the bottom shelves. The accessories and other equipments like surgical instruments, rubber goods and sutures should be stored separately on racks specially reserved for the purpose. Cash counter and wrapping counter should be near the gate.

There is no specific rule by which the drugs should be arranged in a store. It depends on the individual who is to handle the store. The arrangement should meet his and the institutional requirements. Generally the drugs may be arranged according to their categories or according to the companies who have supplied the drugs, but they must be arranged alphabetically on the shelves.

Legal requirements to start a drug store

The sale of drugs is quite different from the sale of ordinary goods. For ordinary goods the consumer can select the goods according to his own choice whereas in the case of drugs neither the patient himself nor the chemist can select the drugs but the choice of drugs for a particular patient is in the hands of the physician or the doctor. Moreover the sale of drugs is a technical job which must be performed by a qualified person. Whenever a drug store (retailsale or wholesale) is to be opened, there are certain legal requirements which must be fulfilled.

(i) Minimum qualifications

A person who is interested to start a retailsale drug store must be a registered pharmacist with State Pharmacy Council. To become a registered pharmacist he or she must have passed Degree or Diploma in Pharmacy from a recognised institution. A person who does not possess degree of diploma in pharmacy qualification may also open a retailsale drug store but the licence for the retailsale of drugs will only be granted to a registered pharmacist employed for the purpose.

A person who is interested to start a wholesale drug store may not be a registered pharmacist but he must have passed at least matriculation examination and must possess four years experience in handling the drugs.

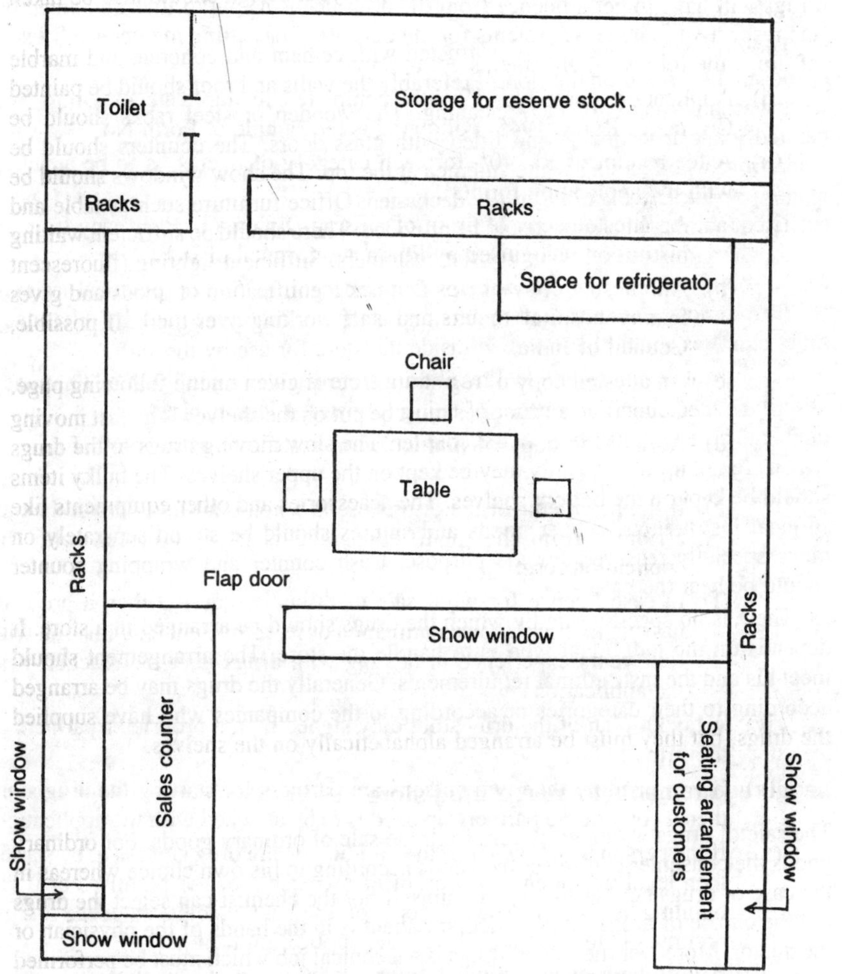

Layout Design of an Ideal Retail Drug Store

(ii) Minimum space

A minimum area of 10 square metres is required to run a drug store which should be equipped with proper storage accommodation for preserving the properties of the drugs to which the licence applies. There should be a sufficient number of racks to store drugs and pharmaceuticals. For the storage of vitamins, antibiotics, vaccines, sera, enzymatic preparations etc. a refrigerator is necessary to store such drugs at a temperature between 2°C to 8°C so as to preserve their potencies.

(iii) Application for the grant of licence

Any person who wants to sell, stock, exhibit or offer for sale or distribute the drugs will have to get a licence from the drug licensing authorities appointed by the respective State Governments for the purpose. For getting the licence for sale of drugs the following documents are required :

(i) Application Form No. 19 duly completed in duplicate of Drugs and Cosmetics Rules, 1945. Following is the sample of Form No. 19.

(ii) A fee receipt of Rs. 40/- for each category of licence is to be attached with the application form(s).

(iii) (a) An attested copy of proof of passing Diploma in Pharmacy from an institution recognised by Pharmacy Council of India.

(b) An attested copy of proof of undergoing 750 hrs. practical training in any hospital or chemist shop as recommended by Pharmacy Council of India.

(c) An attested copy of registration certificate issued by State Pharmacy Council as a proof of being Registered Pharmacist.

(d) An attested copy of matriculation certificate as a proof of date of birth.

(e) If the proprietor of the drug store is a non-qualified person then an affidavit from the qualified person is to be attached with the application form.

(f) In case licence for wholesale of drugs is required then a proof of passing matriculation examination or its equivalent examination with four years experience in dealing with drugs is to be attached with the application.

(iv) A layout plan of the drug store duly signed by the proprietor/partners of the firm.

(v) If two or more than two persons are partners for starting the drug store then a copy of the partnership deed is to be attached with the application.

(vi) If the person is the owner of the building where drug store is to be started then legal documents as a proof of ownership of the premises or if the building is on rent then a copy of the rent receipt/rent deed of the premises is to be attached with the application form.

(vii) An affidavit of non-conviction under Drugs and Cosmetics Act on Rs. 3/- non-judicial stamp paper, duly attested by a first class magistrate is to be attached. In case of proprietorship concern the proprietor himself

"FORM 19"
[See Rule 59 (2)]

Application for grant or renewal of a licence to sell, stock or exhibit for sale or distribution of drugs other than those specified in Schedule X

I/We .... hereby apply for licence to sell by Wholesale/Retail Drugs specified in Schedule C and C_1 excluding those specified in Schedule C, C_1 and X to the Drugs and Cosmetics Rules, 1945 and also to operate a pharmacy on the premises situated at ....

2. The sale and dispensing of drugs will be made under the personal supervision of the qualified persons, namely :

(Name) .... (Qualifications) ....

(Name) .... (Qualifications) ....

3. Categories of drugs to be sold Biological/Non-Biological

4. Particulars for special storage accommodation Refrigerator/Racks

5. A fee of Rupees 40/- (Rs. forty only) has been credited to the Government account under the Head of account.

0210 - Medical & Public Health
01 - Urban Health Service
800 - Other Receipts
Renewal of Drugs Licence Fee

Dated .... Signature ....

and in case of partnership concern each partner will submit the above mentioned affidavit along with the application form.

All the above mentioned documents are to be attached with the application form and submitted to the drug administration authorities. After scrutinising the application form and documents if all the requirements are fulfilled, then the drug control authorities will personally visit the premises for which the licence for sale of drugs is required. If the authorities are satisfied then the licence for the sale of drugs may be issued on the following forms as the case may be :

(a) Form No. 20—Licence to sell, stock or exhibit or offer for sale or distribute drugs by retail other than those specified in Schedules C and C_1.

(b) Form No. 20 B—Licence to sell, stock or exhibit or offer for sale or distribute by wholesale, drugs other than those specified in Schedules C and C_1.

(c) Form No. 21—Licence to sell, stock or exhibit or offer for sale or distribute by retail, drugs specified in Schedules C and C_1.

(d) Form No. 21 B—Licence to sell, stock or exhibit or offer for sale or distribute by wholesale, drugs specified in Schedules C and C_1.

Following is the sample of Form No. 20 and 21.

FORM 20
[See Rule 61 (1)]

Licence to sell, stock or exhibit or offer for sale or distribute drugs by retail other than those specified in Schedules C and C_1.

1. .... is hereby licensed to sell, stock or exhibit (or offer) for sale or distribute by retail drugs other than those specified in Schedules C and C_1 of the Drugs and Cosmetics Rules, 1945 and to operate a pharmacy on the premises situated at .... subject to the conditions specified below and to the provisions of the Drugs and Cosmetics Act, 1940 and the rules thereunder.
2. The licence shall be in force from .... to ....
3. Name(s) of qualified person(s) in-charge ....
4. Categories of drugs ....
5. Licence No. ....

Date ....   Licensing Authority

Conditions of Licence

1. This licence shall be displayed in prominent place in a part of the premises open to the public.
2. The licence shall comply with the provisions of the Drugs and Cosmetics Act, 1940 and the Rules thereunder for the time being in force.
3. The licencee shall report to the Licensing Authority any change in the qualified staff incharge within one month of such change.
4. No drug shall be sold unless such drug is purchased under cash or credit memo from a duly licensed dealer or a duly licensed manufacturer.
5. The licencee shall inform the Licensing Authority in writing in the event of any change in constitution of the firm operating under the licence. Where any change in the constitution of the firm takes place, the current licence shall be deemed to be valid for a maximum period of three months from the date on which the change takes place unless, in the meantime, a fresh licence has been taken from the Licensing Authority in the name of the firm with the changed constitution.

FORM 21
[See Rule 61 (2)]

Licence to sell, stock or exhibit or offer for sale, or distribute by retail drugs specified in Schedules C and C_1.

1. .... is hereby licensed to sell, stock or exhibit (or offer) for sale or distribute by retail the following categories of drugs specified in Schedules C and C_1 of the Drugs and Cosmetics Rules, 1945 and to operate a pharmacy on the premises situated at .... subject to the conditions specified below and to the provisions of the Drugs and Cosmetics Act, 1940 and the Rules thereunder.
2. The licence shall be in force from .... to ....
3. Name(s) of qualified person(s) incharge ....
4. Categories of drugs ....
5. Licence No. ....

Date ....   Licensing Authority

Conditions of Licence

1. This licence shall be displayed in a prominent place in a part of the premises open to the public.
2. The licencee shall report to the licensing authority any change in the qualified staff incharge within one month of such change.
3. If the licencee wants to sell, stock or exhibit for the sale, distribute, during the currency of the Licence, additional categories of drugs listed in Schedule C and C_1 but not included in this licence, he should apply to the licensing authority for necessary permission. This licence will be deemed to extend to the categories of drugs in respect of which such permission is given. This permission shall be endorsed on the licence by the Licensing Authority.
4. No drug shall be sold unless such drug is purchased under cash or credit memo from a duly licensed dealer or duly licensed manufacturer.
5. The licencee shall inform the Licensing Authority in writing in the event of any change in constitution of the firm operating under the licence. Where any change in the constitution of the firm takes place, the current licence shall be deemed to be valid for a maximum period of three months from the date on which the change takes place unless, in the meantime, a fresh licence has been taken from the Licensing Authority in the name of the firm with the changed constitution.

Sale at more than one place

If drugs are sold or stocked for sale at more than one place, separate application shall be made, and a separate licence shall be issued in respect of each such place.

Duration of licence

The original licence or a renewed licence to sell drugs, unless suspended or cancelled earlier shall be valid up to 31st December of the year following the year in which it is granted or renewed.

Renewal of licence

An application along with the prescribed fee is required to be made before the expiry of licence or within six months after the expiry of the licence along with late fee, the licence shall continue to be in force until orders are passed on the application. The licence shall be deemed to have expired if the application for renewal of licence is not made within six months after its expiry.

Manpower requirement of a drug store

Generally the manpower of a drug store depends on the type of store (retailsale or wholesale), sale turnover, space of the drug store and financial position of the drug store. For a medium size drug store the following manpower is required:

(i) Owner or manager
(ii) Salesman and two counter salesmen
(iii) Two delivery boys
(iv) One clerk
(v) One part-time or full time accountant
(vi) Driver of the vehicle

(i) Manager

Basically it is the duty and responsibility of the owner or the manager to look after the whole business regarding purchasing, storing, distributing, supervising the staff and planning all these activities in the best possible way. He will also see the financial aspects of the business which is the most important factor in smooth running of the business. The success of the firm will mainly depend on him, his leadership and sound planning.

Basically the manager of the firm should be a graduate or diploma holder in pharmacy who should have sufficient knowledge of pharmaceuticals and other business activities. However persons from other faculties who have sufficient skill and knowledge can also work as manager. It is seen that some persons who were employed as salesmen, delivery boys, clerks or accountants have risen to the status of managing director of the firm on account of their hard work, grasping of knowledge, sincerity and honesty.

(ii) Salesman/counter salesman

Salesman who will go to the market and meet various retailers should be energetic, influential, skillful and possess sufficient knowledge about pharmaceuticals. He should have marketing skill to create demand so as to book orders. He should be wise and tactful to collect the repayments promptly from the customers to whom the goods were sold on credit.

Counter salesman should be a pharmacy diploma holder who should be smart, well dressed, soft spoken, sincere and honest. He should have sufficient knowledge and be able to read and understand the prescriptions written by the doctors. He should be able to reply the quarries made by customers.

(iii) Delivery boys

The main work of the delivery boys is to deliver the goods on the premises of the customers either against the orders already booked by the salesmen or against the orders placed on the spot. The additional job of the delivery boys include packing the orders, storing the goods on racks, cleaning the goods etc. and any other work assigned by the proprietor/salesmen.

(iv) Clerk

One clerk is required for writing the cash and credit bills transferring the bills on creditor's accounts regularly, placing the orders with suppliers, typing the letters and reminders. Sometimes clerks are assigned to do the bank works like depositing the cash/cheques withdrawal from banks, getting the demand draft prepared from the bank etc.

Clerk should be at least matriculate (preferably a graduate) fluent in English writing and typing work.

(v) Accountant

Depending on the workload one accountant on part-time or full time basis may be employed to maintain the accounts, enter bills in credit or debit accounts, prepare balance sheet and trial balance etc. The accountant should be B.Com, or M.Com having experience of accounts.

(vi) Driver

Depending on the nature of vehicle driver(s) is required to supply the drugs to other wholesalers, retailers and user departments. The vehicles employed for this work may include bicycle, rickshaw, autorickshaw, scooter, delivery van etc.

Importance and Objectives of Purchasing

Purchasing is one of the important functions of material management. Purchasing may be defined as the procurement of materials, supplies, machinery, tools and equipment and services required to produce certain goods. It also includes the planning and policy activities, research and development and selection of source of supply etc.

According to Dr. Walter, "Scientific purchasing means procurement by purchase of the proper materials, machinery, equipment and supplies or stores used in the manufacture of a product, adopted to marketing the proper quantity and quality at the proper time and at the lowest price consistent with the quality desired."

All the business organisations i.e. manufacturers, wholesalers and retailers buy the goods in one form or the other. The manufacturers buy the machinery, tools and equipment, raw materials and services whereas wholesalers and retailers generally buy the finished goods. In fact, the whole success of any business organisation depends on effective buying. Therefore all big industries usually employ expert buyers to look after effective buying.

Functions of Purchase Department

Basically the word buying not only involves purchasing of goods but involves the entire purchase procedure i.e.

1. Assessing total material requirement.
2. Deciding the economic order quantity i.e. the optimum number of units or quantity that must be purchased under one order.
3. Market surveying i.e. to find out the best sources of supply at reasonable cost.
4. Calling for quotations and tenders.
5. Placing the order for the required quantity on the basis of quotations or tenders according to the terms and conditions laid therein.
6. Receiving the goods and inspection thereof both quantity and quality-wise.
7. Sending the goods to store.
8. Checking the bill and making the payment.
9. To dispose of the outdated and damaged articles.
10. To see that the duplication in purchase is avoided and materials are not wasted or damaged by the user departments.
11. To settle the disputes connected with the purchase of materials.
12. To maintain records regarding suppliers, products available with them, their dealings in the past etc.

Types of Purchasing

(a) Centralised Purchasing

When the entire raw materials requirement is purchased at the central point for the whole company, it is known as centralised purchasing.

(b) Decentralised Purchasing

Under this method each different user department makes its own purchasing.

Objectives of Purchasing

The basic aim of purchase is to ensure continuous supply of raw materials, tools and equipments and machinery without any time gap in the right quality and quantity at reasonable costs. The following are the main objectives of purchasing :

(i) Right quality

Whenever any material is to be purchased its specifications must be given in the supply order preferably in terms of market grade, brand or trade names, chemical or physical characteristics or name of the manufacturing company e.g. ordinary grade, laboratory grade or analytical grade by BDH, SM, Ranbaxy etc. This will facilitate the supplier to supply the materials according to the specifications as desired by the users.

(ii) Right quantity

It is wise to purchase the materials in the right quantity because the purchase of any kind of material needs investment therefore it should be purchased only in the required quantities. There is no use of purchasing the goods in large quantities at a time which will block the money. Therefore concepts such as Economic Order Quantity, and Economic Purchase Quantity must be considered which will serve as broad guidelines. For purchasing the materials the purchase manager has to use his knowledge, experience and common sense to determine the quantity to be purchased which also depends on factors like price structure, discount, availability of items etc.

With consultation of other departments the purchase manager will decide which item is to be purchased and in what quantity is to be purchased which will be sufficient to run the business.

(iii) Right price

The items should be purchased at the lowest price at no compromise with the quality. This can be done by inviting the quotations or tenders from different suppliers and then comparing the rates of the items. The order can be placed with that supplier whose rates are lowest. Some of the suppliers give different types of incentives like quantity discount, trade discount, cash discount etc. which should also be taken into consideration while deciding the lowest rate of the suppliers.

(iv) Right time

Time of purchase is a very important factor in purchasing. The items should be purchased in such a way that they remain with the chemist or the manufacturer for the minimum period of time because so long they will remain with the chemist the money will remain blocked. Moreover the goods may deteriorate with the passage of time.

(v) Right source

The source of supply should be dependable and capable of supplying the items of uniform quality at presettled price.

(vi) Right modes of transport

The purchase department is to see that which mode of transport will be most suitable so as to deliver the goods at right place and at right time. The goods may be supplied by road, rail, air or sea.

Purchase Procedure

The different steps involved in the purchase of goods is known as purchase procedure. A systematic purchase procedure is very important for the smooth running of the organisation. The purchase procedure generally involves the following steps :

(i) Determination of purchase budget.
(ii) Determination of material requirement.
(iii) Finding the source of supply.
(iv) Inviting quotations or tenders.
(v) Opening the quotations or tenders.
(vi) Placing the order.
(vii) Receipt of materials and inspection.
(viii) Checking the bills and releasing the payment.

(i) Determination of purchase budget

Overall purchase budget of the company is prepared out of which every user department is allocated funds for the purchase of their requirements. If allocated surplus funds are present then the purchase for that department will be affected otherwise not. In case of urgency the purchase will be done by diverting the funds from other departments.

(ii) Determination of materials requirement

The purchase department requests the various user departments to send their requirements on a proper requisition form in which the items, its specifications, quantity to be purchased and approximate costs are mentioned.

After receiving the requisition forms from user departments, the purchase department consolidates the requirements to know the total quantity of each item to be purchased.

(iii) Finding the source of supply

A list of suppliers is prepared from market survey, journals, newspapers and trade journals. The suppliers are selected who are honest, can supply the materials in time and in the desired quantities. About the nature of suppliers the information can be collected from own past experience as well as from fellow businessmen. Whose performance is bad in regard to quality, delivery, sale price etc. should be removed from the list of suppliers.

(iv) Inviting quotations or tenders

Quotations are invited by supplying the list of requirements to the suppliers who are existing on the list of suppliers. The tenders may also be invited by publishing the list of requirements in leading newspapers. A fixed date is given up to which the quotations or tenders must reach to the purchase department.

(v) Opening the quotations or tenders

On the due date and time all the quotations or tenders received are opened by the committee constituted for the purpose. The persons who have submitted their quotations or tenders may present themselves, if they so desire, at the place of opening the quotations. After opening the quotations a comparative statement for all the suppliers is prepared. The supplier who has quoted the minimum rate for the required specifications is selected for placing the order. Similar procedure is adopted for each and every item. While preparing the comparative statement there are various points which must be taken into consideration. These points include price, quality, quantity, time period during which supply will be made, mode of delivery, imposition of various taxes, trade discount, mode of payment etc.

(vi) Placing the order

Once the suppliers are selected on the basis of comparative statement, the order(s) is placed for the required items to the respective supplier. For placing the order a standard supply order form is used. In this form the detailed specifications of the items, quantity required, the price and other terms and conditions are mentioned. This type of standard supply order form is commonly known as "Supply Order". The supply order is signed by an authorised person and serves as a legal document between the buyer and the supplier.

The number of copies of supply order to be prepared varies from organisation to organisation. Generally 3-5 copies are prepared.

(a) The original copy is sent to the supplier.
(b) The second copy is sent to the store.
(c) The third copy is sent to the accounts section.
(d) The fourth copy is retained by the purchase department.

After receiving the supply order it becomes the duty of the supplier to supply the materials in time but if the materials are not supplied within the stipulated time then follow-up letters may be sent so that the purchase is affected. But if the supplier does not supply the materials at all then he may be blacklisted and in future he may not be sent any supply order.

(vii) Receipt of materials and inspection

The materials sent by the suppliers are received in the store. Then each and every item is physically inspected for its quality and quantity and compared with supply order as well as challan form, invoice or bill sent by the supplier. If the goods received do not conform to the specifications mentioned in the supply order, there is variation in price, there is any breakage or shortage or there is any other discrepancy that must be recorded on the challan form or bill and the supplier must be informed immediately about the same so as to remove the discrepancies pointed out.

(viii) Checking the bills and releasing the payment

After verifying the quality and quantity and arithmetical accuracy the bill is sent to the accounts section for releasing the payment. Generally the payment is made to the concerned supplier through crossed cheque or draft.

Mode of Purchasing

(i) By inspection
(ii) By sample
(iii) By description
(iv) By grading.

(i) By inspection

This is the oldest mode of purchasing and is still widely used in retail and wholesale transactions. Under this method the detailed examination of goods regarding their quality and price are made.

(ii) By sample

In this method the purchasing is done by examining the sample of goods which represent the entire quantity of the goods to be supplied.

(iii) By description

Certain products become popular by advertisement due to brand name or trade names given to them. These types of goods are purchased simply by description and price described in catalogues.

(iv) By grading

Purchasing of standard quality items are done by grading e.g. grade A milk, C grade iron pipe, special grade apples, ISI grade, Agmark grade, I.P. grade, B.P. grade, U.S.P. grade etc. This method is usually used for future trading of uniform and standard products.

Selection of Suppliers

The prospective suppliers are contacted through their sales representatives, their catalogues and sample of items, through the advertisements appearing in newspapers, trade journals, trade directories, trade shows and trade conferences. When a new item is required to be procured for the first time and the source of supply is not known, the best way would be to advertise the demand. A number of suppliers may respond to this advertisement. Amongst these the suitable one is selected.

Factors responsible for the selection of prospective suppliers

(i) The sample is according to the required specifications.
(ii) The price is lowest or reasonable as compared to the competitors.
(iii) Response to the quotations invited is prompt.

(iv) Past performance specially in the time of shortage or emergency requirement.

(v) Financial position of the supplier i.e. can he supply the materials on credit or not.

(vi) Can he supply the required consignment according to the delivery schedule.

(vii) Will he provide after sales service and technical assistance or not.

(viii) His general behaviour, co-operation, attitude with regard to the goods rejected and returned by the purchaser and reputation in the market.

Taking into consideration the above mentioned factors a list of favoured suppliers is prepared which will be used for future purchases as well. Such lists of suppliers for different categories of items are prepared because no one supplier will be able to supply all kinds of items.

Credit Information

No businessman is willing to give the goods on credit because of the fear of bad debts. But credit is very important in order to increase the sales of the organisation. A business cannot flourish unless the goods are sold on credit.

To establish and make hold in the market a newly developed organisation will have to sell the goods on credit but once the organisation makes hold in the market then it may or may not give the goods on credit. Credit becomes important both for the sellers as well as the buyers. For giving the goods on credit a well defined policy is formulated regarding the amount of credit sales, number of days for which credit is given, interest to be charged on credits etc. Goods cannot be sold on credit to every buyer. For such sales various factors are taken into consideration such as :

(a) Reputation of the customer in the market.

(b) Capacity of the customer to repay.

(c) Analysis of the financial statements of customer.

(d) Liabilities of the customer.

(e) Total time period of existence of the concern in the market.

Some of the pharmaceutical manufacturers give 45 days credit from the date of invoice bill to the well established wholesalers but the new wholesalers are not given the credit facility. They will have to get the bilties of consignments through a bank after paying the amount. Similarly a wholesaler also gives 15 to 21 days credit to the retailers after establishing the business relationships with them. Credit facilities are not given to those retailers who are not good pay masters and who do not follow time schedule. Generally the well established organisations and whose products are fast moving do not sell the goods on credit. They prefer cash sales.

TENDERS

After receiving the requirements from user departments the next step of the purchase department is to purchase the materials. For this purpose the quotations or tenders are invited from the list of reputed suppliers who are approved by the purchase department. A tender or a quotation is a written offer to do some specified work or to provide the required materials. Such an offer is accompanied by certain conditions like time period up to which the tenders must reach to the purchase department, quantity required or nature of work to be completed etc.

Types of Tenders

There are four types of tenders out of which the purchase department may invite any kind of tender given below :

1. Single tender
2. Closed tender
3. Open tender
4. Global tender

1. Single tender

Sometimes the material required is of specific nature and only one supplier is there as in the case of patent and proprietary goods. In such cases the supplier is asked to send his quotations along with terms and conditions of supply. So the tenders invited from one supplier is known as single tender.

2. Closed tender

Closed tender is also known as limited tender system because in this case the tenders are invited from a limited number of suppliers who are on the approved list of suppliers. Supply orders are given to those suppliers who have quoted the minimum rates for the specified item. When more than one supplier has quoted the same rate with same specifications of the item then the order may be placed to the most reputed supplier.

3. Open tender

Open tender is also known as public tender or unlimited tender system because in this case tender is not limited to certain suppliers. In open tender a wide publicity is given by advertising the tender notice in various newspapers and trade journals. Open tenders are invited when :

(a) Large quantities of materials are required.
(b) Huge costs are involved.
(c) Large scale work is to be done.
(d) Sources of supply are not known.

The open tender system is very common in government departments. Here the suppliers are asked to apply on the tender form, available at certain cost from the purchase department of the concerned office/company. In the tender notice as well as tender form various conditions such as last date of receiving, date and time of opening, place of opening, quantity required, period and place of delivery, specifications and other terms and conditions for supply are mentioned.

The suppliers who are interested to supply the materials will fill the tender form and submit the same within the specified date and time to the concerned department. The representative example of an open tender is given below :

Tender Notice

Sealed tenders are invited by the undersigned for the supply of drugs and intravenous fluids from the manufacturers/authorised distributors for the supply of above mentioned items (the detailed list is attached with the tender form) for the financial year 1996-97 so as to reach the office of the Director Health Services, Chandigarh Administration, Chandigarh.

The prescribed tender form and other detailed N.I.T. specifications etc. can be had from the office of the undersigned on any working day between 10 A.M. to 4 P.M. up to 5.8.1996. The last date of receipt of tenders is up to 2 P.M. on 6.8.1996 and shall be opened at the same time in the presence of the tenderer or their authorised representatives who would like to be present at that time.

Sr. No.	Description	Approximate cost	Earnest money	Time limit
1.	Drugs	2.0 lac	10000/-	One month
2.	Intravenous fluids	1.0 lac	5000/-	One month
3.	Surgical dressings	50000/-	2500/-	One month

The tender must be accompanied by earnest money. No tender will be accepted without earnest money.

The tender should be sent in a sealed cover with marking "Tender for the supply of Drugs and Intravenous fluids" due on 6.8.1995 at 2.0 P.M. addressed to the Director Health Services, Chandigarh Administration, Chandigarh.

The rates should be quoted FOR destination, including all taxes, if any.

The supply should be completed within one month from the date of supply order.

The tenders can be accepted/rejected without assigning any reason by the competent authority.

Sd. Purchase Officer

4. Global tender

When materials of international standards are to be purchased or work involving huge costs is to be done then tenders are invited from all parts of the world. Tenders invited in this way are known as global tenders. Generally for the purchase of materials, machines and equipment required for research and scientific work, global tenders are floated.

Opening the Tenders

After receiving the tenders in the concerned office, they are then sent to the purchase department. All the tenders received are entered in the register meant for quotations or tenders. Only those received in time are considered whereas those received late are rejected and remarks given on the tender envelops as well as tender register "Tender received late, hence rejected".

For opening the tenders generally a committee is constituted. This committee opens the tenders in the presence of tenderers or their representatives, if they so desire. All the committee members sign each and every envelope, page, cuttings/overwritings and entries of tenders in the tender register. The entries marked "Received late" are also signed.

At the time of opening the tenders, the purchase officer writes on each tender the Sr. No. of that tender/total number of tenders received/total number of pages in that particular tender e.g. 8/10/5, it means this tender is 8th out of total 10 tenders received and it contains 5 pages in all. By doing so the chances of missing any tender or any page of the tender during handling are eliminated.

Comparative Statement

After opening the tenders a comparative statement of all the tenders is prepared on the following proforma :

Comparative statement for the purchase of equipment for the year 1996-97

N.I.T. No. .... Date of receipt of tender ....

S. No.	Description	Quantity received	Firm No. 1	Firm No. 2	Firm No. 3	Firm No. 4	Remarks
1.							
2.							
3.							
4.							
5.							
	Terms and conditions		1 2 3 4	1 2 3 4	1 2 3 4		

Sd. Sd.
Prepared by Checked by

From the comparative statement so prepared the purchase officer can immediately come to known which firm has quoted the lowest rate for that particular item. Considering the lowest rate and other terms and conditions the order may be placed to that firm who has quoted the minimum rate. The order is placed on the supply order form duly signed by the purchase/authorised officer.

Contracts

When an adequate quantity of material is required to be supplied at regular interval of time or a big job is required to be finished in a considerable length of time is known as contract. The person who agrees to do these jobs is called a contractor and the person who gives the contract for the job is called a contractee.

Contracts are mainly given for large scale works for example canteen contract, mess contract, building contract, roads contract, bridge contract, milk supply contract etc.

The contractor supplies the materials or finishes the work according to the terms and conditions laid down in the contract. The contract agreement is signed by both the parties i.e. the contractee and the contractor and this signed agreement serves as a legal document.

Price Determination

The term price is defined as the amount of money which a buyer pays to a seller for a product or services rendered by him. As the number of services will increase the price of services rendered will also increase. So in other words price can be defined as the amount of money which is needed to acquire a product with or without accompanying its services.

Pricing is a very important factor in the marketing management. The success of any business mainly depends on the fixation of right price of the product. If the prices kept are too high the customers may not like to buy the products and the business may be lost but on the other hand if the prices are kept too low, the firm may not be in a position to earn profits and meet their financial requirements hence the firm may be in loss. Therefore pricing the products is a very important factor for the success of the organisation but it is a very difficult task to determine the right price of the product. Price is a very important factor for both the buyer and the seller. If the price of the product is reasonable the buyers would like to buy the product which will help the seller to earn profits hence firm's competitive position and its share in the market will improve.

As explained earlier also, drugs are not ordinary items, they are special commodities meant for sick persons. Therefore the price of drugs must be reasonable so that every body can afford to buy the drugs. Taking this point into consideration as well as that the traders do not indulge in undue profiteering of drugs the Government of India passed an order known as Drug (Price Control) Order, 1970. This order was passed with a view to ensure equitable distribution of essential bulk drugs and to fix the maximum retail price of drug formulations in order to check profiteering tendencies of the traders.

Since drugs are special commodities so not only they require special storage conditions but specially trained person is required for their dispensing. So all these factors must also be taken into consideration while deciding the price of a drug.

Calculation of retail price of formulations

The retail price of a drug formulation is generally calculated by applying the following formula :

$$RP = (MC + CC + PM + PC) \times \left(1 + \frac{MAPE}{100}\right) + ED$$

where RP = Retail price; MC = Material cost which includes the cost of drugs and other pharmaceutical aids used including averages if any and process loss thereon in accordance with such norms as may be specified from time to time; CC = Conversion costs as per norms notified by the Government from time to time; PM = Cost of packing material; PC = Packing charges; MAPE = Maximum allowable post-manufacturing expenses which include manufacturer's margin, promotional expenses, outward freight, distribution costs and trade commissions (MAPE shall not exceed 100% for indigenously manufactured scheduled formulations); ED = Excise duty.

The retail price should be marked on the label of each container with the words "Retail Price not to exceed ..., local taxes extra". No retailer can sell it to a customer more than its retail price mentioned on the label of the container.

Codification

All the manufacturers, distributors and wholesalers have to keep a large number of goods in the stores. It will be very difficult to locate the items in the store unless some system is evolved to store them. So there should be place for everything and everything should be in its place. Therefore for easy identification and location of various items they are allotted code numbers.

Codification is defined as the process of assigning a code number or code symbol to a particular material for easy identification. According to another definition "Codification is a system of symbols designed to be applied to a classified set of items."

Advantages of Codification

(i) It helps in quick identification of items.
(ii) It helps in grouping the similar items together.
(iii) It helps in avoiding duplication of items.
(iv) It helps in avoiding confusion caused by long descriptions.
(v) It helps in inspection of materials.
(vi) It helps in physical counting.
(vii) It helps in computerisation of stores records and accounting.

Methods of Codification

The following methods of codification are used by various organisations :

1. Alphabetical method
2. Numerical method
3. Alpha-numeral codification
4. Location coding
   (i) Fixed location
   (ii) Random location
   (iii) Zonal location

1. Alphabetical method

According to this system of codification, alphabetical symbols or letters are used to identify an item. Since alphabetical letters are used so this method is also known as letter code system. The first alphabet of each name of the material is the starting point of codification and subsequently sub-alphabets are also used. For example for tablets code T is used and for capsules code C is used. For Tablet Thiamine Hydrochloride Code T-TH-HC and for raw material of Thiamine Hydrochloride TH-HC are used. Similarly for other drugs such alphabetical codes are used. Though this method is very simple to use but it is not suit ble for a large scale organisation where large number of items are to be stored as the number of alphabets are limited. So this method is useful when few types of items are to be stored.

2. Numerical method

This system is also known as scientific method of codification. According to this system the items are divided into a number of groups and each group is given a specific code. Further sub-grouping is done on the basis of classification of items falling in any group according to its shape, size, weight and functions etc. and subcode number is allotted. Then complete code of the item is written by combining the main group code with the subcode of that item.

Specific code numbers are given to a group of drugs acting on a system and subcodes are allotted to each drug falling under this group. For example drugs acting on cardiac system are allotted 01 and individual drugs falling under this group like Atenolol, Ramipril etc. are allotted code as 01.1 and 01.2 respectively and so on. Similarly antibiotics are allotted a code say 02 and drugs falling under this group like Tetracycline, Erythromycin, Ampicillin, Cloxacillin etc. are allotted code as 02.1, 02.2, 02.3 and 02.4 respectively and so on. In this way all categories of drugs can be codified. Because of simplicity this is one of the most widely used system of codification.

3. Alpha-numeral codification

In this method both alphabets and numerals are used in the combined form to allot a code to different items of the store. This method is used where store items are quite large. By this method the code of different store items can be easily remembered.

4. Location coding

In a large organisation there are a large number of stores and each store may be quite large in size. So the store rooms are divided in blocks and each block is identified by lateral block letter and a longitudinal block letter. Within each block every row is divided vertically into columns and horizontally into shelves. Each and every shelf is given a particular number. The location of item can be identified from warehouse number, block number, row number, column number, rack number and shelf number etc. Location of any item inside the store room can also be done in the following manner :

(i) Fixed location

In this method each and every group of items is allotted a fixed place inside the store according to either (a) supplierwise (b) itemwise or (c) according to the utility of the item.

(ii) Random location

This is the most widely used system in almost all kinds of retail shops but each group of items are stored on a particular shelf for its easy location. In this system the shopkeeper or the retailer should be very efficient in remembering the location of each item.

(iii) Zonal location

According to this system the available space is divided into different zones and each zone is allotted to different kinds of items. The zones can be named as (a) bulk zone, (b) reserve stock zone, (c) consumable items zone, and (d) spare parts zone etc.

Handling of drug stores and other hospital supplies

Drug stores

Drug stores are the places where the drugs are stored for distribution to the hospital wards and other user departments. They are handled by competent and legally qualified pharmacists assisted by trained personnels.

Objectives

Drug store has the following objectives :

1. To stock all drugs and accessories required in the hospital.
2. To procure drugs from the different sources.
3. To supply drugs to the consuming departments.
4. To store drugs required in research work.
5. To preserve certain categories of drugs.
6. To maintain records of receipt and issue of drugs.
7. To carry out all the operations regarding drugs economically to save revenue.

Layout and facilities

The medical stores should be centrally located in a spacious and well ventilated building. The rooms should be fitted with shelves and drawers made up of wood or steel. Space should be provided for a refrigerator. A trolley should be provided for transporting heavy articles.

In order that the pharmacist may properly supervise the storage of drugs, they should be stored in an area directly under his control. In this way he will be able to arrange the stocks according to his knowledge as well as according to the prescribing trends of the staff. All the procurements made by pharmacy should directly reach the pharmacy area. If the merchandise are received by the hospital post office or central store room, it should be immediately forwarded to the medical stores in the unopened state. After receiving the merchandise in the stores, the pharmacy personnels are required to check the materials physically with the receiving slip and with the copy of the purchase order. The material received must be entered in the receipt register.

All the medicines and accessories must be put on the shelves. The fast moving items must be kept handy near the counter. The slow moving drugs or the drugs which are not used frequently may be kept on the upper shelves. The bulky items should be kept on the bottom shelves. The accessories and other equipments like surgical instruments, rubber goods and sutures should be stored separately on racks specially reserved for the purpose.

There is no specific rule by which the drugs should be arranged in a store. It depends on the individual who is to handle the store. The arrangement should meet his and the institutional requirements. Generally the drugs may be arranged according to their categories or according to the companies who have supplied the drugs, but they must be arranged alphabetically on the shelves.

The most popular and convenient method is to store the drugs and other hospital supplies according to manufacturer-wise. The drugs are stored in such a way that the older stocks are sold first. The drugs having date of expiry should also be sold before the actual date of expiry otherwise the old stocks and expired drugs will remain unsold resulting in financial loss to the drug store. Such losses can be prevented by placing the old stock in the front rows and the fresh stock on the back rows. The expired drugs must be stored in a separate cupboard meant for storing the expired drugs.

Procedure for Procurement of Drugs and Supplies from the Medical Stores Depot

The drugs and supplies are procured from the Medical Stores Depot (M.S.D.) by the hospitals, institutions and stores by sending the requisition to the depot manager of the Medical Stores Depot. Four copies of the requisition are prepared on the prescribed indent forms supplied by the Medical Stores Depot. Each and every item have been allotted V.M.S. No. (Vocabulary of Medical Stores No.) which must be given while filling the indent form. Complete specifications and unit pack size must also be mentioned. If specifications regarding drug items are not mentioned then the Pharmacopoeial standard drugs are supplied to the indentors.

Three copies of the indent form are sent to the Medical Stores Depot and fourth copy is retained by the indentor. After verifying the stock position of the stores, two copies of the indent are sent back to the indentor mentioning the price of the drugs etc.

After the amount is deposited in advance by the indentor with the Medical Stores Depot, the drugs are supplied to the indentor. On receipt of the drugs/supplies, the materials are verified by the indentor regarding the quality and quantity. Then they are entered into the receipt register and the drugs/supplies stored in the stores.

Procurement of Drugs from Manufacturers/Distributors

Drugs can be procured directly from the manufacturers who are on the list of approved suppliers. Three copies of the requisition are prepared. One copy is retained by the indentor and two copies are sent to the manufacturer. Complete specifications, unit pack size and price must be mentioned according to the list of drugs/materials supplied, from time to time, by the manufacturers.

After receiving the orders, the supplies are made to the indenting department, institution or hospital by the manufacturer. On the receipt of the drugs/supplies the materials are verified by the indentor regarding the quality and quantity of drugs supplied. If found correct, a certificate is given and bills passed for payment. The drugs/supplies are entered in the receipt register and stored in stores.

Some manufacturers do not supply the drugs directly to the user departments but they appoint their own distributors who supply the drugs to indenting departments. The procedure regarding the procurement of drugs/supplies is the same as described in the procedure for procurement of drugs from manufacturers.

Procurement of Drugs from Local Market

The drugs and materials which are urgently required or are required in small quantities can be purchased from the local market by an authorised person against cash payment or credit.

Procedure and Limits for Emergency Purchases

Emergency purchases of drugs are made when they are not in store and they are urgently required. The prescriber must mention that these are life saving drugs and are urgently required for a particular patient and for a particular disease. Only then the drugs are purchased from the local market against cash payment or credit. A pharmacist must be authorised to do the emergency purchases as and when required.

REVISION QUESTIONS

(A) Multiple choice questions

Select the right answer and put the correct word in the respective squares given below :

1. The qualification for starting a retailsale drug store should be :
   (a) Matriculate (b) 10 + 2 with science
   (c) Registered pharmacist
   (d) D. Pharmacy from an unrecognised institution
2. Selection of site for a drug store is a :
   (a) Significant decision (b) Insignificant decision
   (c) Immaterial factor
3. Retailsale drug store can be started with a minimum area of :
   (a) 150 sq. ft. (b) 90-100 sq. ft.
   (c) 200 sq. ft. (d) 70-80 sq. ft.
4. A drug store opened near traffic light or road circle :
   (a) Is a health hazard

(b) Obstructs the customers to visit the shop
(c) Creates parking problem for the customers
(d) Leads to accidents

5. Opening of a drug store in a big city is possible :
(a) If large number of employees are available
(b) With limited financial resources
(c) With only a huge investment
(d) None of the above

1	2	3	4	5

(B) Very short answer type questions

Define the following :

(i) Drug house
(ii) Codification
(iii) Lead time

(C) Long answer type questions

1. What do you understand from the term drug house management? Discuss the factors which should be taken into consideration for the selection of site of a retailsale drug store.
2. Describe layout design of a drug store along with its flow diagram.
3. A pharmacist is interested to start a drug store. Discuss the legal requirement for the same.
4. What do you understand from the term purchasing? Describe importance and objectives of purchasing.
5. Explain the purchase procedures in detail.
6. Write short notes on the following :
   (a) Modes of purchasing
   (b) Selection of suppliers
   (c) Credit information
   (d) Tenders
   (e) Contracts
   (f) Calculation of retail price of a drug formulation.
7. Explain the term 'Codification'. Discuss advantages and methods of codification.

Answers

1	2	3	4	5
c	a	b	c	c

5

Inventory Control

Inventory means all the raw materials, spare parts, tools, maintenance consumables, fuels, lubricants, semiprocessed materials and finished goods etc. recorded in the books of an organisation at any given point of time. On an average about 30% of total working capital is spent on inventories. Therefore it is very important that for the smooth working of the business organisation a sound inventory should be maintained. It should neither be excessive nor inadequate but it should be of optimum level.

There are a number of definitions of inventory but according to one definition, "Inventory is a detailed list of those movable items which are necessary to manufacture a product and to maintain the equipment and machinery in good working order. The quantity and value of every item is also mentioned in the list."

It can also be defined as a systematic control over maintenance of stock in the store department.

Inventory control is an effective way to keep control over losses from misappropriation, damage, deterioration, evaporation and carelessness. This is necessary because investment in materials constitutes a major portion of the cost of production and therefore a strict control has to be kept on inventory.

Objectives of Inventory Control

The main objectives of inventory control are :

1. The producer should supply the items produced to the customers according to their demand i.e. as and when they require. So production will have to be done according to the time of demand. This will only be possible if the raw materials required for production are available in the stores.
2. With properly planned production only the required quantities of material will be stocked in the stores and there is no need to keep the materials in excess quantities which will lead to blocking the money. So with proper planning blockage of money can be saved.
3. With proper planning of production men, machines and materials can best be utilized by keeping them engaged. During slack period the number of workers can be reduced whereas in boom periods the manpower can be increased. Thus money can be saved.
4. With proper control of inventories the materials can be purchased well in advanced by inviting the tenders or calling the quotations and not by purchasing the materials in the nick of time, thus saving money in purchases.
5. With proper planning of production the wastage and surplus can be

reduced because now a days fashions and tastes of people are changing every next day so materials should be cautiously stored so as to prevent the wastage due to change in fashion or change in policy by the government. Sometimes the government bans the production and distribution of certain drugs which will lead to financial losses if those kinds of drugs are stored in bulk in the stores.

6. Having control over the inventories the theft of small but costly items can be checked. For example in a pharmaceutical industry the theft of vitamin B_{12} (even in small quantity) will cost too much to the industry. Similarly in electronics industry the components are very small but very costly which can be easily stolen. With inventory control such thefts can be checked.

From all the above mentioned points it is clear that with proper inventory control production can be streamlined, manpower, machinery and materials can be best utilized, thefts can be checked hence the overall cost of production can be reduced and more profits can be achieved.

Importance

1. Major part of finance of an industry is spent on inventories. If inventory is controlled then the industry can earn more profits.
2. Wastage of materials and theft of materials can be checked.
3. If inventory control is maintained then there are no chances of over-stocking, low-stocking or out of stock of materials in the stores.
4. Men, machines and materials are properly utilized.
5. The products can be supplied to the consumers at a short notice as and when the demand is received.

Methods of Inventory Control

The following methods are used to control the inventory :

1. Perpetual inventory control system.
2. ABC method of inventory control.
3. VED analysis.
4. Lead time.
5. Stock levels.
6. Economic order quantity.

1. Perpetual inventory control system

This system enables the manufacturer to know about the actual position of materials available in the stores without undergoing the difficult task of physical stock verification. Under this system proper examination with regard to receipt, issue and balance of material in hand is being done and every time a receipt or issue is made the entire stock is rechecked. However the success of this system depends on the proper implementation of the process of continuous stock verification. Stock verification may be done daily, weekly, monthly or yearly. The work is more simplified if the data is fed to the computer. The balance of each item can be obtained as and when desired.

Advantages of perpetual inventory control system

1. On account of continuous stock verification the balance in stock can be known at any time during the year.
2. It is helpful in formulating proper purchase policies since position of stock is known.
3. A detailed and more reliable check is obtained.
4. Errors and shortages of stock are readily discovered and efforts are made to avoid the shortage in future.
5. Continuous stock verification will make the storekeeper more vigilant and efficient.
6. Capital investment in materials will be under control.
7. It makes available correct stock figures for claims to be lodged with the insurance company in case of damage.

2. ABC method of inventory control (always better control method)

According to this method the manufacturing organisations divide their materials into three categories according to their respective values. Normally group A constitutes costly items which are 10 to 20% of the total items but has more than 50% of total value of goods. Group B consists of items which constitutes about 20 to 30% of the total items and represent 30% of total value of stores. Group C consists of about 70 to 80% of the items but having only 20% or less percentage of the total value because they are cheaper items. Group A goods are preserved with a greater degree of control. Only necessary quantities of these items are purchased and stocked so as to minimise the investment on these items. Group B items are given a reasonable care whereas group C is only given a routine care.

Advantages of ABC methods of inventory control

1. It ensures better control over costly items.
2. It helps in developing scientific method of controlling inventories.
3. It helps in maintaining the stock in a better way.
4. It helps in reducing the storage costs.
5. It helps in maintaining enough stocks of group A, B and C items.

3. VED analysis

VED system of inventory control is very useful for drugs and consumer goods. Similarly in the industries it is very useful system for spare parts and raw materials. That means it is based on the utility of the goods and materials. According to this system the items are generally classified into three categories i.e.

V stands for vital

E stands for essential

D stands for desirable

Vital items are those items which are of extreme importance for running the shop or industries though the cost of these items may be high or low. So such items must always be available in stock because such items can be demanded at any time.

Essential items are those items without which the production may come to a standstill so such items may have to be purchased at a short notice. Preferably essential items should be available in stock.

Desirable items are those items which are necessary but do not cause any immediate loss in production. Such items need not be stocked in the stores but may be arranged from the market which may cause minor disruptions for a short duration. The motive of this system is to reduce investment in inventories.

In the case of drugs generally drugs are available under a number of brand names. The drugs which are fast moving i.e. which are in great demand should be stocked more than the drugs occasionally demanded and lastly the drugs which are rarely demanded should be stocked in the minimum quantity. In this way the investment in the drug store can be checked and inventories may be controlled in a better manner.

4. Lead time

Lead time is the time gap between placing the order for purchase of certain items to the time of materials are actually received at the stores. Lead time has two components i.e.

(a) Administrative or servicing lead time
(b) Supplier's lead time.

(a) Administrative or servicing lead time

Administrative or servicing lead time is the time taken by the administration for placing the order which includes time taken for calling the quotations, preparing comparative statements, inspecting the materials and then placing the orders. Administrative lead time is also known as internal lead time.

(b) Supplier's lead time

The time gap between the placement of order to the receipt of goods in the store is known as supplier's lead time.

The purchase department must know that how much time is taken for placing the order and within how much time the supplies will be received in the stores. Determining the accurate lead time is very important factor in inventory control. Orders should be placed in advance in such a way that at no time the materials should be out of stock in the stores. If this thing happens then the production may come to stand still and the business may go into losses. Therefore a great care should be given to the lead time. The longer the lead time, the larger is the safety stock required resulting in excess investment in inventories. It may not be possible to decrease the supplier's lead time because it is in the hands of suppliers but internal lead time can be decreased to a desired extent. Therefore the lead time should be decreased to the minimum to keep the investment in inventories within limits. For a retailsale as well as wholesale drug store the lead time is very important to be considered.

5. Stock levels

The motive of inventory management of any organisation is to provide an uninterrupted supply of materials to the production department but at the same time the investment in materials are also kept to the minimum possible extent. These objectives can be achieved by maintaining the following stock levels :

(a) Minimum stock level or safety stock.
(b) Maximum stock level.
(c) Reordering level.

(a) Minimum stock level or safety stock

A minimum stock level means that a minimum quantity of any item or material must be present in stock at all times in order to maintain the production. If the stock decreases below the minimum stock level then there are chances that the production may stop. In order to save such a situation to arise all the production houses maintain a minimum quantity of stock so that the production is not affected due to non-availability of materials. To meet the emergency or exceptional conditions of production some extra stock of materials is maintained which is known as safety stock or buffer stock. The minimum stock level can be calculated by applying the following formula :

Minimum stock level = Re-order level – Average rate of consumption × Average time required to obtain fresh delivery

(b) Maximum stock level

Maximum stock level is the maximum quantity of any item or material which should be present at any time in the store. To store more than the maximum stock level may not be financially viable because the capital will be blocked which may be used somewhere else. The main object of fixing maximum stock level is to avoid overstocking and thereby using working capital in a proper way. Overstocking requires more godown space for which extra rent will have to be paid and overhead expenditure is also increased. It may lead to losses on account of deterioration and obsolescence of materials. The maximum stock level is calculated by taking into consideration the following points :

(i) Rate of consumption of materials.
(ii) Lead time i.e. the time gap between placing the order and receipt of materials.
(iii) Amount of working capital available.
(iv) Storage space available.
(v) Seasonal considerations.
(vi) Consideration of Government policies.
(vii) Risks involved due to deterioration, obsolescence, mortgage etc.
(viii) Possibility of fluctuation in prices in the market.
(ix) Economic order quantity.

Maximum stock level can be calculated by applying the following formula :

Maximum stock level = Re-ordering level + Re-ordering quantity – (Minimum consumption × Minimum re-ordering period)

(c) Re-ordering level

Re-ordering level is the point in between the maximum stock level and minimum stock level at which it becomes necessary to place orders for fresh supplies. The difference of stock between the maximum stock level and minimum stock level should be enough to meet the demand of materials in production till the orders are placed and supplies are received in the stores. Reordering level can be calculated by applying the following formula :

Reordering level = Maximum consumption during the period × Maximum reordering period for delivery

Inventory carrying cost

Inventory carrying cost is the cost involved during holding the inventory per unit time. It includes rent of storage space, cost of racks and bins, maintenance cost, interest on investments, insurance cost, salaries of storekeeper, cost due to obsolescence, deterioration, wastage etc. The larger the volume of inventory, the higher will be the inventory carrying cost and vice versa. In industries a huge amount of money is spent on inventory carrying cost so efforts should be made to reduce the inventory carrying cost by adopting economic order quantity technique.

6. Economic order quantity

Economic order quantity is a technique by which the orders of goods to be purchased are placed in such a way that it gives maximum economy in purchasing of any material. As discussed earlier also that nearly 30 per cent of finance is spent on the cost of material every year. So as far as possible this cost should be reduced to minimum. The quantity of material to be ordered at one time which minimises the cost is known as economic order quantity or optimum order quantity. The total cost of material usually consists of the actual cost of the material, ordering cost and inventory carrying cost. The actual cost depends on the minimum cost as determined by inviting the tenders and quotations. The ordering cost includes the cost of stationery, typing, postage, filing and telephone etc. It also includes the salaries of the staff posted in purchase department, inspection section and accounts section. The inventory carrying cost as discussed earlier includes rent of storage, interest, insurance, cost of racks etc. So the ordering cost and inventory carrying cost must also be taken into consideration while placing the order for purchasing the materials.

At the time of placing the order for the purchase of any material the most important problem is that how much quantity of any material is to be purchased at a time. It should not be too small that frequent purchases are required to be made. In this way ordering expenses will increase and there will be loss of trade discount etc. But on the other hand if the items are purchased in large quantities there will be huge investment on inventories, over stocking and heavy inventory carrying cost. Hence it is clear that if fewer quantities are purchased but too frequently the ordering cost may increase and inventory carrying cost may decrease but on the other hand if large quantities are ordered at a time, the ordering cost may be less but the inventory carrying cost will be too high. Therefore economic order quantity is the most favourable optimum quantity which should be ordered at a time for the purchase of each item because at this point a balance is struck between the acquisition cost and inventory carrying cost. The economic order quantity may be determined by using the following formula :

$$EOQ = \sqrt{\frac{2A \cdot O}{C}}$$

where EOQ = Economic order quantity

A = Annual consumption

O = Ordering cost per unit

C = Carrying cost per unit

Example

For example the annual consumption of a material is 300 units, the cost of material is 30 rupees per unit and ordering cost is 50 rupees per unit. The storage and carrying cost is 10% of inventory value. Find out the economic order quantity and number of orders to be placed per year.

Solution

$$EOQ = \sqrt{\frac{2A \cdot O}{C}}$$

$$\text{Carrying cost (C)} = \frac{30 \times 10}{100} = 3$$

Here A = 300

O = 50

C = 3

By putting the values in the above formula :

$$EOQ = \sqrt{\frac{2 \times 300 \times 50}{3}}$$

$$= \sqrt{\frac{30000}{3}} = 100 \text{ units}$$

$$\text{No. of orders} = \frac{\text{Total consumption}}{\text{EOQ}}$$

$$= \frac{300}{100} = 3 \text{ orders in a year}$$

It means 3 orders with a gap of 4 months each in a year may be placed for the procurement of required materials.

SCRAP AND SURPLUS DISPOSAL

Scrap

Scrap may be defined as the residue obtained during manufacturing process which cannot be reused in that manufacturing process but it may be used either in the same manufacturing house but in different kind of manufacturing processes or in some other factory where such scrap is used as raw material e.g. iron scrap is used in re-rolling mills, paper scrap is used in cardboard mills and plastic scrap is used in various plastic manufacturing units.

Scrap is generated in almost all kinds of manufacturing and service units. In a drug manufacturing house the scrap may arise in the form of powder and fine granules during tablet manufacturing, spoiled capsule shells, empty barrels, cardboard boxes, packaging wooden cases, broken glass bottles, spoiled raw materials, rejected components, defective parts, obsolete material and equipment etc.

The percentage of scrap arising out of total production is a measure of the working efficiency of the employees connected with every aspect of production. If the amount of scrap is more than the normal percentage then it may be assumed that something is wrong either with the machinery or with the manufacturing process or with the employees working over there. So abnormal waste and scrap must be checked periodically and measures should be taken to control the abnormal waste and scrap. This can be done by holding regular meetings with the foreman and his staff. The scrap is usually of small value and it will not fetch as much income as effective production. Thus the cost of production will increase and it may not be possible to sell the products at a competitive price in the market.

Surplus

Surplus material may be defined as that excess stock which is in excess than the normal requirement of a drug store or a drug manufacturing house. The surplus stock may arise due to following reasons :

1. Over estimation regarding anticipated production which did not materialise due to any reason.
2. Faulty planning.
3. Faulty buying.
4. Excessive buying.
5. Improper warehousing facilities.
6. Fault in machinery which may not be corrected for a long time.
7. Due to obsolescence and changing trends in the market.
8. Due to change in government policies.

Disposal

It is advisable that before initiating the disposal process the different kinds of scrap and surplus should be segregated according to the quality, quantity, metal and size. Some of the segregated items may yield better price. Various procedures adopted for the disposal of scrap and surplus are as follows :

1. Scrap may be sold directly to the re-processing industries where such scrap is used as a raw material.
2. Scrap may be sold to scrap dealers through auction.
3. Costly machinery and spare parts may be sold to other similar organisations.
4. Surplus materials should be offered to the original suppliers who may accept the material and pay good amount for that material.
5. Surplus material may be given to similar user departments at a lower price than that of market price.
6. Surplus materials may be donated to charitable organisations.
7. Surplus materials may be auctioned through public auction.
8. If there is no way out for disposal of scrap and surplus then it may be dumped in the dumping place.

REVISION QUESTIONS

(A) Multiple choice questions

Select the right answer and put the correct word in the respective squares given below.

1. Inventory includes :
   (a) Raw materials, spare parts, maintenance consumables etc.
   (b) Salaries of staff (c) Assets and liabilities
   (d) (a) and (b)
2. On an average the amount of capital spent on inventory is about :
   (a) 60% (b) 50%
   (c) 30% (d) 10%
3. The items which represent about 10% to 20% of the total inventory but consume 70% of the total budget of inventory are called :
   (a) Group A items (b) Group B items
   (c) Group C items (d) None of the above
4. A drug store is called an ideal drug store if its inventory is :
   (a) Inadequate (b) In excess
   (c) In between minimum and maximum level
   (d) None of the three
5. Inventory is a :
   (a) Significant part of cost (b) Insignificant part of cost
   (c) Negligible part of cost (d) None of the above
6. In VED analysis V stands for :
   (a) Very good items (b) Very important items
   (c) Vital items (d) (a) and (b)
7. Scrap and surplus disposal helps to :
   (a) Get more funds (b) Reduce investment
   (c) Make available space (d) All the above

1	2	3	4	5	6	7

(B) Matching type questions

Match the items of Column I with appropriate items in Column II.

Column I	Column II
(a) The cheaper items of group C constitute about	(i) maximum economy in purchasing
(b) The old fashioned items are called	(ii) carrying cost and ordering cost
(c) Economic order quantity gives	(iii) obsolete
(d) Economic order quantity aims at minimising	(iv) 70% to 80% of items

a	b	c	d

(C) Very short-answer type questions

(a) Define the following terms :
- (i) Inventory
- (ii) EOQ
- (iii) Danger level
- (iv) Lead time
- (v) Scrap and disposal

(b) Write the full forms of the following :
- (i) ABC
- (ii) EOQ
- (iii) VED

(D) Short-answer type questions

1. Write the main objectives of inventory control.
2. Discuss perpetual inventory control system. Describe its advantages.
3. Describe various functions of inventory control.
4. Write short notes on the following :
   (a) Perpetual inventory control system
   (b) ABC method of inventory control
   (c) VED analysis
   (d) Lead time
   (e) Economic order quantity
5. Explain the procedure to be followed for the disposal of surplus items.
6. Write the formulas for determining :
   (a) Minimum stock level
   (b) Maximum stock level
   (c) Reordering level
   (d) Economic order quantity

(E) Long-answer type questions

1. What do you understand from the term "inventory"? Describe objectives and importance of inventory control.
2. What is inventory control? Discuss various methods of inventory control.
3. Define the term "scrap" and "surplus". Discuss how surplus stock may arise and explain methods of its disposal.
4. What do you know about EOQ? Discuss how EOQ can be calculated.

Answers

(A)

1	2	3	4	5	6	7
d	c	a	c	a	c	d

(B)

a	b	c	d
(iv)	(iii)	(i)	(ii)

6

Sales Promotion

The main aim of any business is to earn maximum profit so as to raise the standard of business organisation as well as for future expansion of the business. This is possible only by increasing the sales. There are various techniques by which the sales can be increased to great extent which include personal selling, advertising and publicity. Sales promotion is another technique of raising the sales other than personal selling, advertising and publicity but includes window display, free samples, premium on sales, dealer incentives, demonstrations, patient counselling, drug information service, fairs and exhibitions.

According to American Marketing Association, "Sales Promotion" refers to those activities other than personal selling, advertising and publicity that stimulate consumer purchasing and dealer effectiveness such as displays, shows and exhibitions, demonstrations and various other non-recurring selling efforts not in the ordinary routine.

Sales promotion techniques are short-term incentives given to customers to motivate and encourage them to purchase the product or services. These techniques are more commonly used for sales promotion of consumer goods, grocery items, toilet, cosmetic preparations and household remedies. These techniques are used only to some extent in the sales promotion of drugs because for drugs the doctor is to decide what kind of medicine is to be given to the patient. Neither the patient himself nor the chemist can decide the medicine to be purchased or sold.

Objectives of sales promotion

Sales promotion techniques are used for the following objects or purposes :

(i) To introduce new products in the market.

(ii) To attract new customers and maintain old ones by satisfying their requirements.

(iii) To improve image of the store in the minds of the public.

(iv) To stabilise fluctuating sales and increase sales during slack season.

(v) To improve product visibility at sales counter through counter display or window display.

(vi) To create demand in the minds of the public so that they may purchase more items.

(viii) To clear inventory of old products and making room for the new products as is done by arranging clearing sales.

(viii) To help salesmen and the dealers.

Techniques or methods of sales promotion

There are a large number of techniques by which sales can be promoted. Every business house has its own sales promotion techniques which are targeted to customers, dealers or salesmen. Following are the most commonly used techniques of sale promotion :

(i) Free samples
(ii) Lower price
(iii) Extra quantity
(iv) Premium or bonus offer
(v) Coupons
(vi) Trading stamps
(vii) Dealer gifts
(viii) Consumer contests
(ix) Dealer display contests
(x) Trade allowance
(xi) Fairs and exhibitions.

As mentioned earlier also these sales promotion techniques are more commonly used in consumer goods but only a few out of these techniques are used for sales promotion of drugs.

(i) Free samples

Free distribution of samples is a very powerful technique of sales promotion but it is very expensive and is adopted by big concerns specially when a new product is introduced in the market. Many drug manufacturing houses send their medical representatives to the doctors for detailing and distribution of free samples. Regular size packages or special sample size packages specially prepared for free distribution are given to the doctors along with the literature of concerned product.

After going through the literature if the doctor feels it worth prescribing then he prescribes the product to his patients. Distribution of free samples to doctors is the most widely used system of sales promotion of drugs.

In the case of consumer goods the free samples are distributed by sales girls from house to house, in retail stores, on stalls, exhibitions or fairs. The common products for free samples include household remedies, cosmetic preparations, toilet preparations, kitchen items etc. Though it is an expensive method but even then commonly used.

(ii) Lower price

Under this method some of the manufacturers sell their products at lower price than the original price so as to attract customers to buy more quantities and to promote sales. This is very common technique in off seasons and festival seasons. The shopkeepers offer different kinds of attractive schem
tempted to buy the products.

(iii) Extra quantity

This is also a good technique of sales promotion of goods. Under this method the manufacturers offer more quantity of the product at the same price or with a nominal increase in price. This technique is quite commonly used in the case of detergents, tooth pastes, cosmetics, tea, jams, sauces and Ayurvedic products.

(iv) Premium or bonus offer

In this technique the manufacturers offer certain amount of product or any other kind of incentive to the buyer at no extra cost to the buyer who buys a specified quantity of product. The premium offered to the buyers may be in the following forms :

(i) Premium offer along with the pack.
(ii) A reusable container
(iii) A free in the mail premium.

(i) Premium offer along with the pack

The incentive article may be inserted in the package of the product or attached outside the package or it can be given separately over the counter. For example a stainless steel spoon may be inserted along with the cough syrup bottle in the package; a tooth brush along with tooth paste pack, a packet of sugar along with 500 gm of tea pack etc.

(ii) A reusable container

In this technique the product is packed in an attractive and reusable container. A reusable container is that container which has utility to the consumer after the product is used. Many kinds of products are packed in such types of containers. For example Chyawanprash, Horlicks, Eno salt, baby foods, dry milk, dry fruits, coffee, toffees, jams, detergents etc. are packed in reusable attractive containers made of glass, plastic or tin which can be reused in the kitchen. Now a days it has become the general trend of manufacturers to pack the products in reusable containers.

(iii) Free in the mail premium

The manufacturers give certain incentives to the buyers who send either the cash memo or the wrappers of the containers of a particular product to the manufacturer who in turn sends some kind of gift by post to the purchaser. Sometimes the manufacturers direct the purchaser to collect his gift from a specific shop authorised to do so.

(v) Coupons

Coupon is a certificate that entitles its holder to a specified saving on a specified product. Such coupons may be inserted in the package, distributed directly through mail, newspapers, magazines or through the retailers over the counter. The holder of the coupons can buy the product at concessional rates from retailers. Some of the companies distribute coupons to its shareholders who can purchase the items at specified concessional rates. For example Vimal, Raymonds, Gwalior Suitings, Digjam, Bombay Dyeing etc. distribute coupons to its shareholders. The retail showrooms of respective companies honour these coupons and deliver the items at fixed discounts. The coupons so collected by the retailers are passed on to the company who reimburses the value of coupons and also pay certain percentage of money as handling charges to the dealers. Generally the retailers other than company showroom retail outlets do not like this scheme because it causes financial and accounting problems for them.

(vi) Trading stamps

In this technique trading stamps are issued by the retailers to the customers for a particular period of time on the sale of certain kind of products. During this period the buyer goes on collecting these stamps on his purchases until he has a sufficient number of stamps or at the expiry of time he can get a free product in exchange of his stamps. Certain manufacturing houses also issue such schemes e.g. sometime back Coca Cola and Thumps Up cold drinks floated a scheme that whosoever will collect 100 crowns of particular brand will get four filled bottles free of cold drinks of that particular brand. Similarly Nestle and other companies go on floating such schemes from time to time.

(vii) Dealer gifts

Attractive gifts are given to dealers who will place order in bulk for the products. Otherwise also free gifts are distributed to retailers during festival seasons so that they may promote the sale of that company.

(viii) Consumer contests

In consumer contests the consumers are asked to write a slogan for a particular product. Such contests are held through radio, TV, newspapers, magazines etc. Lucky draws are held for best entries and attractive prizes are distributed to the winners.

(ix) Dealer display contests

The dealers are asked to display the goods of a particular company in their retail outlets in show windows or otherwise in the shop. The dealer with best display of the product(s) is awarded. The idea behind such contests is to create awareness among consumers about the product and to push sales. Certain drug manufacturing houses arrange such dealer display contests for cough syrups, analgesics, G.I.T. preparations etc.

(x) Trade allowance

Wholesalers as well as retailers are given trade allowances in the form of cash discount, bulk order discount, display discount etc.

(xi) Fairs and exhibitions

On fairs and exhibitions the manufacturers can display their products and demonstrate by explaining their special features and usefulness. Pharmaceutical manufacturers take advantage of fairs and exhibitions held at medical, dental, homeopathic, ayurvedic and pharmaceutical conferences, seminars and science fairs. On such occasions the firms can distribute literature to introduce their firm and products to the public. For consumer goods such exhibitions are arranged off and on. Various state governments encourage their entrepreneurs to participate in such exhibitions and display their products. Government of India arranges industrial trade fairs every year in which manufacturers from different states and other countries are also invited to participate.

For sales promotion it is not necessary that all the manufacturers will adopt the same technique(s). It is up to them that which method is suitable to them by which their sales can be promoted. From time to time the manufacturers also go on changing their sales promotion techniques.

Salesmanship

The ultimate aim of any business organisation is to earn profits to run and expand the organisation. The profit directly depends on sales; higher the sales higher will be the profit. In order to achieve higher sales targets a businessman has to adopt various techniques to increase the sales. Salesmanship or personal selling is one of the most important techniques of enhancing the sales.

Salesmanship is the oldest and common method of selling. Unlike advertisement and publicity, salesmanship relies on personal contact that is to say that salesmanship is the process of creating demand and promoting sales by assisting and persuading the prospective buyer to buy a particular items in a face to face situation. In other words salesmanship involves three stages viz. (a) information, (b) persuasion, and (c) sales.

The real purpose of salesmanship is not to induce or trap innocent people to buy which they do not require or cannot afford but to guide them and to educate them about the finer qualities of the product, remove their misunderstandings and to build up permanent demand and goodwill of product.

According to Garfield Blake, "Salesmanship consists of winning the buyer's confidence for the seller's house and goods, thereby winning regular and permanent customers."

Importance of salesmanship

1. It helps in increasing the sales and bringing larger profits to the businessman.
2. It helps in convincing and persuading a prospective buyer to buy particular goods.
3. It helps in creating demand for new products.
4. It is very helpful in raising the living standards of the people by creating demand for luxury goods.
5. A salesman can satisfy the customers by showing different articles best suited to the needs and pocket of the customers.
6. It provides employment opportunities to young and energetic people.

7. It provides market information to the manufacturers which is quite helpful in regulating the production.

Salesman

A person who sells the goods to customers is known as salesman. In olden days it was the general tradition that son(s) used to adopt the profession of his father hence they used to learn the sales techniques from his father but now a days the selling techniques have undergone a sea charge. A person who wants to adopt selling as a carrier will have to undergo intensive coaching and training. The success of any firm mainly depends on its salesmen. Therefore, it is extremely necessary to engage well qualified, trained, honest, energetic and young persons as salesmen of the company.

Types of salesmen

The salesmen are classified according to their employers which are discussed as follows :

(i) Manufacturer's salesmen
(ii) Wholesaler's salesmen
(iii) Retailer's salesmen

(i) Manufacturer's salesmen

These types of salesmen deal only in a limited number of products manufactured by that manufacturer. They possess highly specialised and extensive knowledge about all those products which they have to explain to the customers. Generally they deal directly with the middlemen and collect bulk orders from them and pass on the same to the manufacturer.

(ii) Wholesaler's salesmen

They work for wholesalers and generally deal with retailers or industrial consumers. These salesmen may be outdoor salesmen or indoor salesmen. The outdoor salesmen go out in the market and explain to the retailers about the new products available, stocks readily available, new techniques of sales promotion, various types of concessions given to retailers as well as to consumers and book orders from the retailers.

The indoor salesmen work on the shop itself where they receive the retailers and supply the products required by them. They also help the wholesaler in the other kinds of activities like loading, unloading, counting and checking the articles and bank works etc. as desired by the wholesaler.

(iii) Retailer's salesmen

Retailer's salesmen generally deal with the actual consumers. Therefore, it requires special kind of training and technique to deal with different kinds of persons. He will have to receive, attend and serve the customers in a courteous and polite manner so as to win their goodwill and sell the products desired by them.

Qualities of successful salesman

A successful salesman should have the following qualities :

1. Physical attributes

(a) **Good personality :** He should have a pleasing and charming personality, good habits, well dressed, fine way of presenting himself and polite way of addressing others.

(b) **Sound health :** Salesman should be physically fit and have no handicap like stammering, limping or any other kind of physical handicap.

(c) **Good stamina :** He should have a good stamina to work hard over a long period of time and must not get exhausted very soon.

2. Mental attributes

(a) **Alertness :** He should be very alert and should quickly respond to any queries made by the other party.

(b) **Imaginative and tactful :** He should be imaginative and tactful in handling the unresponsive customers.

(c) **Persuasive and convincing nature :** He should be able to persuade and convince the buyer regarding the usefulness of the product and he should help the customers in selecting the products best suited to their needs.

Sometimes even after lot of persuasion and convincing the customers do not buy anything, they merely waste lot of time of the salesman asking for more and more variety of products. In such cases the salesman should not lose temper rather he should try to satisfy the customers and win their confidence.

In certain cases the customer raises the objections about the product or has the impression in his mind that the product of some other manufacturer is better than yours then the salesmen must be able to answer the questions raised by the customer and should be able to satisfy him and convince him to buy the product.

(d) **Sharp memory :** He should be able to recognise his customers even if he meets them after a long time.

(e) **Thorough knowledge of the product :** He should know the exact composition, uses and price of the product. He should also have knowledge regarding its manufacturer.

3. Moral and social attributes

(a) He must be able to deal with people of all types, nature and temperament.

(b) He must be honest and loyal besides having a sound character.

(c) He must be co-operative with fellow salesmen and helpful to customers.

(d) He must be able to converse in different languages especially the local language.

Salesmanship in pharmaceutical industry

Salesmanship of ordinary consumer goods is quite different from the salesmanship of pharmaceutical products because the former is concerned with the seller and the customer whereas the latter is concerned with the chemists and mainly with the physicians who are to prescribe the medicines and not with the customers directly.

The persons who work as salesmen in pharmaceutical industry are known as 'detailmen', 'medical representatives' (MRs) or 'professional services representatives' (PSRs). These persons approach the doctors or the physicians and talk face-to-face and person-to-person and explain to them about the products of their manufacturers. They give detailed information in every respect regarding their products. If the physician considers the products suitable he will prescribe these products to the patients.

The main success of any pharmaceutical manufacturing house depends on well trained team of 'detailmen'. Therefore each drug house has its own organisation which is solely concerned with the sales promotion of the company. Though this method of personal selling is very costly as compared to other methods of sales promotion but even then it is preferred by pharmaceutical companies because it has many advantages such as :

1. A detailman has direct talks with the physician and can explain to him in a nice way. Moreover he can answer the specific questions of the physician immediately.
2. A detailman visits the physician every week and explains to him about the introduction of new products and reminds him about the existence of old products. From the talks with the physician a detailman can understand the prescribing trend about his product which is immediately passed on to the manufacturer for future planning.

Selection of detailmen or medical representatives

Since the success of any pharmaceutical manufacturing house mainly depends on the working of their medical representatives so they should be selected very carefully. For the selection of a good medical representative he should have the following qualities :

1. He should have pleasing and charming personality and well dressed.
2. He should be polite and have fine way of presenting himself to others.
3. He should be physically fit and have no stammering or limping.
4. He should have competitive spirit.
5. He should have good stamina to work.
6. He should be able to travel over long distances.
7. He should be alert and tactful.
8. He should have lot of patience.
9. He should be hard worker, honest and loyal to his work.
10. He should have sharp memory.
11. He should have up to date general knowledge.
12. He should have sound character.

13. He should be able to converse in different languages specially the local language.

Training of detailmen

As discussed earlier also the success of any pharmaceutical company depends on its detailmen and the success of detailmen depends on their training. Therefore the newly appointed graduates or experienced hands from other companies are given extensive training by the medical and research staff of the company under the direction of the 'sales training department' specially created for the purpose.

All the detailmen of the company are given training to make them fully conversant with products of their company as well as the products of the competing companies. They are told about the differences of their formulations, testing and standardisation from same type of products of other companies so that they may explain these points to the physician and be able to reply to their questions. They are also given training in sales techniques and company policies. Apart from initial training, a continuous training is imparted to detailmen at specified intervals of time to keep their knowledge up to date regarding the products of the company as well as continuously changing trends of the market. So training of detailmen is a continuous process which goes on throughout their sales carrier.

Compensation or remuneration of detailmen

For the services rendered by the detailmen to the company they are compensated by giving remuneration in one or more of the following ways :

1. A fixed salary or running scale.
2. Some commission or bonus on sales promotions.
3. Reimbursement of expenses like boarding and lodging, travelling allowance, daily allowance etc.
4. Additional benefits in cash or kind for achieving the fixed sales targets.
5. Reimbursement of petty expenses.

Advertising

The word 'advertising' has been derived from the Latin term 'advertere' which means turning the attention towards the product. Advertisement may be defined as the art of making a business establishment and its products known to the public in such a way that a desire is created in the minds of the people to buy that particular product. According to Frank Prespray advertising may be defined as "Advertising is printed, written, spoken or graphic salesmanship. Advertisements are designed to sell the products of the advertiser and to influence favourably the public mind, individually and collectively with respect to the interests of the advertiser."

The main aim of any kind of business is to sell the goods in the maximum quantities so as to earn maximum profit. The success of the business depends on the sales of the organisation. Hence it is the endeavour of every businessman to increase his sales to the maximum extent. To achieve this goal he adopts different methods out of which advertisement is the most important method of persuading the people to buy their products.

In the modern business there is severe competition for capturing market share. Therefore it is necessary that the manufacturer keep the consumer informed about the existence of a product, its additional features, advantages in comparison to other products, place of its availability etc. Now a days not only the manufacturers do advertisement but doctors, lawyers, educational institutions, employers and job seekers also advertise to fulfill their aim. In fact advertisement is becoming an essential feature of modern society therefore becoming more scientific in character.

Objects of advertising

1. To maintain and create demand

With the ever increasing inflow of large manufacturers, it is necessary that the consumers are time and again reminded of the existence of the product and its distinct features. This is possible only through advertisement.

2. To create confidence in the consumers

The big industrial houses, through advertisement are able to create such confidence amongst the consumers that he does not even think of buying another product.

3. Creating pre-launching awareness

Even before a product has been introduced in the market, the advertisement begins which creates acceptance in the minds of the customers who then start waiting for the product e.g. the recent massive advertisement campaign launched by the makers of Pepsi Cold Drinks.

Advantages of advertising

1. It encourages the prospective buyers to purchase the products.
2. It helps in the introduction of new products in the market.
3. It helps the manufacturer in creating permanent demand for the product.
4. To some extent it helps in decreasing the middlemen.
5. For standard products it increases goodwill of the manufacturer in the market.
6. It increases sales by either introducing new products in the market or by telling about the different uses of the existing products.
7. It helps in increasing the turnover of the manufacturers.
8. It provides an important source of revenue to different advertising agencies and publishers of various newspapers and magazines.
9. It gives direct or indirect employment to a number of persons like painters, photographers, singers, cartoonists etc.
10. It helps to raise the standard of living by creating desire in the minds of the people for purchasing better products.

11. It helps the consumer by educating him about the product and thus facilitates decision-making on his part which ultimately gives satisfaction to the consumer by buying that particular product.
12. It helps the salesmen to a great extent because by advertisement more than half the work is done. The salesman now has to merely exhibit the product and sell it.

Disadvantages

1. Excessive advertisement increases the cost of product which is a burden on the consumer.
2. It creates an artificial demand for the product in the minds of the people to buy that product which are not actually needed by them which leads to unhealthy atmosphere in certain families.
3. Sometimes innocent customers are cheated by false advertisements.
4. A huge amount of money is wasted on advertisements.
5. Sometimes it leads to monopoly of certain manufacturers for particular products.
6. Sometimes advertisements are done in indecent language and virtually nude photographs in order to attract the customers which leads to downfall in morality and adversely affect the social values.

Types of advertisement media

There are a large number of advertising media but none satisfy the advertiser because advertisement trend changes daily. Therefore, the advertiser finds new ways and means for advertising their products. Basically the various advertising media used are as follows :

1. Press

Press is considered as a very powerful media to reach a large section of people at reasonable cost. A very strong point in favour of press advertisement is that it can be read time and again and at any convenient time. Due to these favourable points it has been recognised as the primary medium of advertising. Various methods of press advertisement are :

(a) National and regional newspapers
(b) Magazines
(c) Periodicals
(d) Pamphlets and hand bills
(e) Posters.

2. Television

It is a very powerful media of advertisement since visual shots attract the prospective customers and leave effective and permanent impression on the minds of the viewers. This mode of advertisement is becoming more popular day by day although it is very expensive. Actually the television has revolutionised the advertising process.

3. Radio

Before the advent of television, the radio was a very powerful and popular means of advertisement because the message was conveyed to a large section of public, illiterate or educated, and even to remote places.

4. Films

It serves as an audio-visual way of advertisement and is shown as slides or documentary films in cinema houses. It is a costly method of advertisement and only big business houses can afford it. Its coverage is limited and only the local public is benefited.

5. Direct mailing

Direct mailing means that the prospective customers are contacted by post only by sending cards, envelopes, folders, calendars, booklets and catalogues. This method is commonly used in pharmaceutical marketing. A contact is developed with the physicians by sending booklets, catalogues etc. by post. Sometimes reply paid post cards are also sent. In this method a list of physicians, pharmacists, hospitals and research institutions is prepared to whom these materials are supplied. The printed matter supplied should be attractive and interesting. They should also contain brief description and price of the product. By this method of advertisement samples of drugs may also be sent to the physicians.

6. Outdoor publicity

It means advertising through the hoardings, banners, neon sign boards, posters, balloons, etc. However it has to be put at a centralised place where it can be seen by a large number of people. The main aim of outdoor advertising is to catch the attention of passers-by within twinkling of an eye. Specially neon light is an attractive mode of outdoor publicity.

Advertisement of pharmaceutical products

The advertisement of consumer goods and pharmaceutical products is quite different from each other because the former are made directly to the consumers whereas the latter are addressed to the doctors or physicians who are the deciding persons for the selection of a particular medicine for a particular patient and not the patient himself. Similarly the chemist or pharmacist cannot dispense the medicines of his own choice, he will have to dispense only those medicines which are prescribed by the doctor, physician or R.M.P. This is because the drugs and medicines, due to their potencies and toxicities require lot of discretion and judgement in their use which can only be provided by an authorised expert medical person. The direct advertisement of drugs to the public may lead to self medication with very serious results. Due to these reasons the direct advertisement of drugs to public is prohibited. However the advertisement of cosmetics and household remedies can be done for which the above mentioned advertising medias may be adopted.

Recently the WHO has passed a resolution regarding the advertisement of drugs which is as follows :

"The advertisement of pharmaceutical products should be truthful. There should not be any wrong statement regarding its contents and their percentage. It should provide full details regarding the action and uses, proprietary name as well as the generic name, dosage form, mode of administration, side effects, treatment of toxic effects, precautions and contraindications. The above statements should be truthful, scientifically correct and proved."

The advertisement of pharmaceutical products giving above mentioned information is of no use to either patients or chemists. Such advertisements will be helpful only to the doctors, physicians and RMPs. Therefore for the advertisement of pharmaceutical products following media of advertising may be used :

(i) Direct mailing
(ii) Personal contact or detailing
(iii) Professional magazines and journals
(iv) Through video cassettes and other audio-visual medias.

If anybody contravenes any provision of the Act and Rules and indulges in prohibited advertisements may be prosecuted and imprisoned up to six months or a fine or both on first conviction and with imprisonment up to one year or a fine or both on any subsequent conviction.

Window display

It is the most effective and direct method of attracting the immediate attention of the customers. It is the most common method which is usually adopted by retailers. They display and arrange the products in the show window, counter and shelves of the shop in a systematic and decorative way so as to raise curiosity amongst the customers to buy the product. Show window is the index of the shop, therefore, the latest designs and attractive products should be displayed in the show window, which should be changed regularly. Large show windows are also arranged at stations, bus stands, airports and cinema halls etc.

Sometimes leading manufacturers hold competitions for window display and award prizes to winners who arrange the goods in attractive and systematic manner.

Window display attracts the customers into the shop where he can be shown more variety of goods, therefore, high quality, eye-catching and reasonably priced goods should be displayed in the show window. It also helps the hesitating customers to make up their minds to buy certain goods by letting them know both the price and also that a particular product is available in the shop.

As the advertisement of pharmaceutical products is prohibited therefore they are not displayed in the show windows. Only the non-ethical, cosmetics and household products can be displayed in the show windows.

Advantages of window display

(i) It acts as a silent salesman for promoting sales.

(ii) It is a good method of advertisement.

(iii) It makes the shop more decorative and attractive.

(iv) It attracts the customers and passers-by.

(v) It helps the hesitant customers to make up their minds to buy certain goods by letting them know both the quality and price of the product.

(vi) The customers come to know that what kind of products are available in the shop.

(vii) It creates good impression on the customer when he enters the shop.

(viii) It saves time of the shopkeeper.

(ix) It promotes sales.

Market research

The aim of every producer is to sell his products to earn money. This is only possible if he has made up plans regarding the type of pharmaceutical products to be produced, the quantity to be produced and the outlets where the materials produced can be sold. This is only possible if thorough market research has been carried out.

Gone are the days when the producers used to produce the articles simply by guessing the demand of the product in the market. Now a days the customers have become very active, specific and choosy. They do not accept substandard products or the products which are not according to their taste. So production under modern setup is carried out according to consumer demand as the modern concept of marketing is also consumer-oriented.

Market research means to obtain and analyse marketing information regarding the demand of customers, their liking and disliking of the products and what they need from the manufacturing concern. Marketing research is different from market research. Marketing research deals with all the points concerning various functions of the market which include location of the market, nature of the market, product analysis, sales analysis, time, place and media of advertising, personal selling, channels of distribution and warehousing etc.

According to one definition market research is defined as "The systematic gathering, recording and analysing the data about the problems associated with the sale of goods and services from producer to consumer."

Marketing research is a continuous process of gathering various types of informations. Even the past informations are of great help on the basis of which new strategies of work can be chalked out. So marketing research is a very effective tool of knowing and understanding the present and future marketing problems on the basis of which needs of the customers are understood and fulfilled so as to satisfy them. Marketing research is of great use for consumer goods, medicines, industrial goods and services.

In the present world there is a great competition in every field. In business all kinds of businessmen have to face a lot of competition from other competitors. Therefore only those businessmen can survive in the market who are able to compete with other competitors. This shall only be possible if he has done thorough market research and makes his plans and policies by keeping in view the plans and policies of the competitors. All such informations shall be available through market research.

Advantages of market research

(i) It helps in the introduction of new products in the market.

(ii) It helps in collecting the information regarding liking and disliking of the products by the consumers. On the basis of this information the design, colour and other qualities of the products can be altered to make it more acceptable to the consumers.

(iii) It can help in forecasting the market demands which will have direct effect on purchase, and production departments of the factory.

(iv) It helps to find out other similar products available in the market.

(v) It helps to find out the plans and policies of competitors.

(vi) It helps to find out the prescribing trends of physicians.

(vi) It helps in discovering new markets.

(vii) It helps in knowing the behaviour of middlemen towards the policies of the firm. If not suitable to middlemen or consumers the same may be altered accordingly.

(viii) It provides latest information about change in Government policies which may directly or indirectly affect the business of the firm.

Limitations and drawbacks of market research

(i) In market research huge expenditure of money is involved, therefore, all concerns cannot afford it.

(ii) Market research is of technical nature so well trained and experienced persons are required to be entrusted with the job.

(iii) The effectiveness of marketing research mainly depends on the information and data collected from the market.

(iv) The market research is based on the information and data collected by human beings which may not be true. This may affect the plans and policies of the firm.

Sources of market research

The information and data of market research is collected from the following sources :

A. Internal sources

B. External sources

A. Internal sources

Internal sources means that the sources of information and data are present in the company itself in the form of trading and profit and loss account, balance sheet, advertisement and transportation cost etc. These sources provide useful informations for marketing research which can be analysed to get the desired information regarding the market trend.

B. External sources

External sources include :

(a) Primary sources
(b) Secondary sources

(a) Primary sources

When the data is collected from the market by the researcher himself it is called the primary data and the sources from whom this kind of data is collected are called primarily sources. Generally the data so collected is more reliable and accurate. Since it is collected slowly therefore it involves large cost and time. The primary sources of market information include :

(i) Salesmen
(ii) Dealers
(iii) Consumers

(i) Salesmen

Salesmen are the most important source of providing valuable data to the researchers because they are in close contact with the consumers. They can provide first hand information about the buying habits of the customers, likings and dislikings of the customers, changing trends and tastes of customers, preferences of the customers for the products of other competitors etc. In certain cases they can also provide information about the interest of the dealer in particular firms. The salesmen may be asked to prepare periodic reports about such informations which can be collected from them by the researcher. The salesmen's reports and opinions will be of great help to the marketing managers in formulating various policies of the firm. Information provided by the salesman has one drawback that it may not be accurate and reliable as the salesmen may not be efficient and trained for such work.

(ii) Dealers

Dealers are another important source from whom information for market research can be collected. They act as intermediaries between manufacturer and consumer, hence can provide information in more effective manner regarding consumer's reaction to the firm's products, popularity of the firm's products, share of firms products in the market as compared to the share of other competitors and regarding plans and policies of the competitors. Dealers have this drawback that they may not provide correct information with the idea that their secret arrangements with other competitors may not be leaked out or they may not take interest in the affairs of the firm.

(iii) Consumers

Consumers are the best and most reliable source of providing information for market research because they can provide the exact picture regarding the quality, price, packaging, their liking and disliking about the product and reasons thereof, availability of firm's product etc. Their suggestions about the improvement of the products can be recorded. The information so collected from the actual consumers is accurate and most reliable hence very useful for formulating new plans and policies of the firm.

(b) Secondary sources

There are certain government and non-government agencies which collect the information after doing the proper survey of all types of sources then these agencies present the data so collected in the printed form. The manufacturers take advantage of this data in formulating their own plans and policies. In other words secondary sources are those sources in which the data is collected by some agencies but utilized by some other firm for its own purposes. The advantage of secondary data is that it is available at a very low cost and can be collected within a short period of time. The main sources of secondary data include newspapers, journals like Eastern Pharmacist, Indian Journal of Pharmaceutical Education, Pharma Times, Pharma Pulse etc., magazines, bulletins, periodicals, publications of business associations like Trade Association, Chamber of Commerce, Associations of Manufacturers etc., government publications, publications of Reserve Bank of India and financial institutions, foreign government and international agencies like UNO, World Bank and IMF etc.

Methods of conducting market research

As discussed above for market research the secondary data is readily available without spending much money but for collecting data from primary sources independent surveys by each firm will have to be conducted. Since it is not possible to contact all the physicians, retail chemists and patients so only a random survey is carried out and the data so collected is processed for formulating plans and policies.

Survey methods used for the collection of first hand information or primary data include :

(i) Personal interview method
(ii) Postal survey method
(iii) Telephone interview method
(iv) Panel method
(v) Experimentation method

(i) Personal interview method

This is the best method of collecting the data because the researcher can talk face to face with the consumer and note down his answers for the questions put to him or the consumer can be given a questionnaire (a list of questions) which he will answer and return to the researcher. Since this type of survey is conducted from house to house so it is very time-consuming and costly but even then this is considered the best method.

(ii) Postal survey method

In this method printed questionnaire is sent to the concerned persons with a request to supply the written replies. The questionnaire can be sent to a large number of persons scattered throughout the country as well as in foreign countries. The written questionnaire may be sent along with a covering letter and stamped reply envelope to get a quick response. Incentives like gifts may be offered to respondents to ensure quick return of the duly completed questionnaire. Reminders may be sent after waiting for sometime. This method has one drawback that the respondents do not take much interest in such surveys.

(iii) Telephone interview method

In this method selected questions are asked from physicians and dealers about the usefulness of a drug, its prescribing trends etc. Though this method is very quick but has certain limitations that :

(a) The doctors and dealers may not be able to spare much time to give reply to the questions on the telephone.

(b) This method can cover only those respondents who have telephones.

(iv) Panel method

In this method various panels are constituted comprising of a group of persons, families, retailers and wholesalers. These panels provide information about the products and market policies of the firm. The panel members are provided with diaries for noting the information which may be periodically collected from them for analysis or the panel members may be invited at one place and the data is collected by personal discussions.

(v) Experimentation method

In this method before deciding any policy for marketing, experiments are carried out to know the sale potential and marketing trend of any product (specially the newly introduced product). A small lot of the product is sent to the market at a low cost than competitors or as free samples. The distribution of such products may be done through retailers or house to house visit. This is done just to see the consumer's reaction towards the product. If the consumer will like the product he will definitely demand from the retailer and the retailer will place order for that product with the manufacturer. So from the market demand the manufacturer can draw the conclusion about the production on large scale.

The experimentation method is quite useful and frequently used for household remedies and consumer products but it is very costly and time-consuming process.

Though all the above mentioned methods are very useful for collecting the data, no single method is so reliable which will provide full information. Therefore it is better to use more than one method for collecting the data for formulating the plans and policies of the firm.

REVISION QUESTIONS

(A) Multiple choice questions

Select the right answer and put the correct word in the respective squares given below :

1. The main aim of any business is to :
   (a) Gain popularity (b) To give employment
   (c) To earn maximum profit (d) All the above
2. Which of the following modes of advertisement is long-lasting :
   (i) Radio (ii) T.V.
   (iii) Newspapers and magazines (iv) Sign-boards
3. Which of the following modes of advertisement is most suitable for an illiterate person :
   (a) Newspapers and magazines (b) Radio
   (c) T.V. and other audio-visual systems
   (d) None of the above

1	2	3

(B) Very short-answer type questions

(a) Define the following terms :
   (i) Sales promotion (ii) Salesmanship
   (iii) Salesman (iv) Advertising
   (v) Window display (vi) Market research

(b) Name different methods of sales promotion.

(c) Name various methods used for advertising the pharmaceutical products.

(d) Name various sources of market research.

(C) Short-answer type questions

1. What is sales promotion? Describe objectives of sales promotion.
2. Discuss various methods of sales promotion.
3. What is salesmanship? Describe importance of salesmanship.
4. Describe the qualities of a successful salesmanship.
5. What is advertising? Describe various methods of advertisement.
6. Give an account of recruitment, training and compensation of a pharmacist.
7. What do you understand from market research? Describe advantages of market research.
8. Write short notes on the following :
   (i) Sales promotion (ii) Salesmanship
   (iii) Medical detailman (iv) Advertising methods
   (v) Market research (vi) Window display

(D) Long-answer type questions

1. What do you understand from the term "sales promotion"? Describe objectives and various techniques of sales promotion.
2. Describe the terms "salesmanship" and "salesman". Discuss the qualities of a successful salesman.
3. Describe the salesmanship in pharmaceutical industry. How it differs from salesmanship of ordinary goods?
4. What is advertisement? Describe its advantages and disadvantages. Give a brief account of types of advertising media including advertisement of pharmaceuticals.
5. What is market research? How it differs from marketing research? Describe advantages and limitations of market research.
6. What do you understand from the word market research? Describe the sources and methods of conducting market research.

Answers

(A)

1	2	3
c	c	c

7

Recruitment, Training, Evaluation and Compensation of the Pharmacist

Recruitment

Recruitment is the process of giving employment to suitable persons in an organisation. For this purpose the search is made by stimulating and encouraging the prospective employees to apply for job in the organisation. In this way a large number of persons are tempted with the idea to get a job. Amongst the eligible persons suitable person(s) can be selected for the job.

Methods of recruitment

For the recruitment of a pharmacist it is necessary that he should have passed diploma in pharmacy course from an institution recognised by the Pharmacy Council of India; registered as pharmacist with state pharmacy council and must have attained the age of 18 years.

Various methods are adopted to recruit most suitable and prospective pharmacists for pharmacies. Following are a few methods out of which one or more than one method can be adopted for this purpose :

1. By displaying notice on the notice board at the gate of the premises.
2. By advertising in local and national newspapers and professional journals.
3. By sending requisition to various employment exchanges.
4. By inviting the applications through educational institutions.
5. By requesting the present pharmacy employees for recommending the names of suitable candidates.
6. Through professional associations and clubs.

The interested candidates are generally asked to submit their written applications up to specified time by giving such information as name, father's name, address, date of birth, telephone number, educational qualifications, names of schools/colleges attended, experience, if any, with place and nature of work; physical characteristics such as height, weight etc., and pay requirements. All the applications so received are checked and those applicants who fulfill the minimum requirements are called for interview.

Selection

The applicants called for interview are subjected to personal interview to gauge his personality, aptitude, motivation and character. Sometimes before the personal interview, the applicants are given written tests to gauge the intelligence, alertness and general knowledge. Through written tests and personal interviews, right candidates for the job are selected. Sometimes second and third interview may also be conducted for the selection of suitable candidates. The selected candidates are then issued appointment letters and asked to join the duties within specified time.

Training

Training is defined as an organised procedure for increasing the existing knowledge and skills of the employees for specific purposes. Almost all big organisations have their own training centres and training programmes. All kinds of employees viz. unskilled, semi-skilled and skilled workers, supervisory staff, managerial staff and salesmen are imparted training, though nature of training will be different for each category of employees. Similarly pharmacists employed in different fields like dispensing pharmacist, retailsale pharmacist, manufacturing pharmacist, detailman etc. are imparted training according to the nature of duties.

Advantages of training of employees

Training to employees has the following advantages :

(i) Training helps in moulding the behaviour of the newly recruited employees so as to make them conversant with the working of the organisation.

(ii) Training helps in increasing the performance of the employees. A trained worker can handle the work more skillfully than untrained worker thereby there can be increase in quality and quantity of work.

(iii) Properly trained persons can handle the work independently and satisfactorily which will boost his morale and gave him job satisfaction.

(iv) For properly trained workers no supervision or instructions from the supervisor are required.

(v) Untrained workers may waste more material and damage the machines which may result in accidents. But the trained workers will handle the machines more carefully and avoid wastage of materials. In this way rate of accidents will decrease, there will be less wastage of materials and ultimately increase in production and lower costs.

(vi) Training is necessary for old workers to refresh their knowledge about new methods and techniques as well as new machines and equipment.

(vii) Training is necessary to make the field workers and managers conversant with changing trends of the market, change in plans and policies of the organisation as well as the existing and changing plans and policies of the competitors.

For a retailsale pharmacist following subjects should be covered in his

(i) Rules and policies of the drug store.
(ii) Method of arranging the drugs on the shelves, show windows etc.
(iii) Method of preparing the cash memo, maintaining records of sales, maintaining records of store and maintaining cash book.
(iv) Technical knowledge about the existing and new products of different drug manufacturing houses.
(v) Courteous behaviour with the colleagues and customers.
(vi) Dealings with drug authorities and other kind of inspectors.

For the above mentioned subjects, training to the pharmacist is generally imparted by the proprietor, managers and senior colleagues of the organisation.

Evaluation of a pharmacist

After putting 3 months, 6 months or one year service the pharmacists are evaluated for their honesty, behaviour, sincerity, dedication to work etc. This work is done by the employer or chief pharmacist. If the work and conduct of the pharmacist is found satisfactory then his name is recommended for permanent absorption in the organisation. All the pharmacists/workers are evaluated for giving promotions, yearly increments, additional increments and other kinds of benefits to the pharmacists/employees working in the organisation. For this purpose pharmacists can be evaluated on the basis of check list given below.

Ashoka Medical Hall
Section 16, Chandigarh

Proforma of Evaluation

Name of the Pharmacist/Employee :
Age : Sex :
Date of joining :
Experience :

1. Appearance :
2. Personality :
3. Is he alert and prompt in dealing with customers? Yes/No
4. Is he courteous to customers? Yes/No
5. Does he take interest in his work? Yes/No
6. Is he honest? Yes/No
7. Is he hard working? Yes/No
8. Is he co-operative with his colleagues? Yes/No
9. Is he respected by his colleagues? Yes/No
10. Does he work independently? Yes/No
11. Does he give creative suggestions? Yes/No
12. Does he possess leadership qualities? Yes/No

From the above check list grade such as poor, fair, very good, excellent may be given to each employee and then consolidated list is prepared. On the basis of this consolidated list the pharmacists and other employees of the organisation may be granted promotions and other service benefits.

Compensation to a pharmacist

An adequate compensation or remuneration paid to the pharmacists for the services rendered by them have a great influence on the results shown by them. A good and proper compensation secures better pharmacists with dedication of work, greater incentive to increase the sales, higher morale and greater confidence of the pharmacists in the organisation. The methods of compensation differ from organisation to organisation but generally one or more of the following methods are adopted :

1. Fixed salary or running scale.
2. Commission basis.
3. Salary and commission.
4. Salary and bonus.
5. Free accommodation or house rent allowance, free medical aid, children education allowance, travelling allowance, group insurance and leave travel concession (L.T.C.) etc.

REVISION QUESTIONS

(A) Very short-answer type questions

Define the following terms :

(i) Recruitment
(ii) Selection
(iii) Training
(iv) Evaluation
(v) Compensation

(B) Short-answer type questions

1. Describe methods of recruitment of a pharmacist.
2. Discuss how the selection of pharmacists is done.
3. Discuss why training of pharmacists is necessary.
4. Explain different methods of training to a pharmacist.
5. Write in brief about the evaluation of a pharmacist.
6. Give a proforma of evaluation of a pharmacist.

(C) Long-answer type questions

1. What is recruitment? Discuss methods of recruitment and advantages of training of a pharmacist.
2. Explain the term recruitment and discuss various steps involved in the recruitment of a pharmacist.
3. Explain the term "training". Why is it necessary? Discuss the various subjects in which training should be given to a pharmacist.

4. Write short notes on the following :
   (i) Recruitment of a pharmacist (ii) Selection of a pharmacist
   (iii) Training of a pharmacist (iv) Evaluation of a pharmacist
5. What do you understand from the term "evaluation". Why is it necessary to evaluate a pharmacist? Discuss how the services rendered by a pharmacist can be compensated.

8

Banking and Finance

Bank is defined as an institution where transaction of money takes place. The people deposit their extra money than their requirements in the bank in their own account and can withdraw any amount out of the deposits as and when need arises. Businessmen deposit the money in the accounts of other business organisation with whom business transactions are done. Now a days business is wholly based on credit. Whenever a business transaction is made, generally the payment is not made in the form of cash but the same is made in the form of cheque or demand draft or any other form of bank payments. Thus banking is the backbone of commerce and industry as they play an important role in the working of business and in the economic development of a country.

Services or functions of a bank

A bank has to perform the following functions :

A. Primary functions

1. They accept deposits from the public in their own accounts namely (a) savings account, (b) fixed account, and (c) current account. The money can be deposited in cash, cheque or draft. The bank pays fixed rate of interest on these deposits.
2. The banks give loans to needy persons for different purposes e.g. for building houses, for purchasing conveyance, for setting up business or for expanding the existing business. Now a days banks also give loans for higher studies. The banks give loans to the needy persons but they charge nominal rate of interest on the advances made by it. They also give facility to the customers that they can repay the loans in easy instalments.

   The above mentioned loans are given to investors, businessmen and entrepreneurs against personal security, goods, fixed deposits, life insurance policies, national saving certificates, real estate, gold jewellery and other movable and immovable properties. The documents or property etc. against which the loan is advanced are hypothecated to the bank and remain in the custody of the bank till all the loans in principal amount and interest thereon are totally repaid.
3. The banks allow their customers to draw money more than the amount standing to the credit of his account. The excess money drawn in this way is known as overdraft in banking system. The facility of overdraft is generally given to current account holders. However for overdraft a limit is fixed for each and every individual customer beyond which they cannot withdraw the money as overdraft. For example a customer has

Rs. 70,000/- standing in his amount but he issues cheques for Rs. 1,00,000/-. The difference between these two amounts i.e. Rs. 30,000/- is said to be overdraft to his account. He will have to pay the interest at a specified rate on this amount on daily basis.

4. The banks allow cash credit facility to their customers. According to this facility the bank allows their customers to borrow money up to certain fixed limit against some existing security or guarantee. He can withdraw the money at any time according to his needs and can repay it as and when he is able to do so. An interest is charged by the bank on the outstanding amount in his cash credit account and not on the entire amount.
5. The banks issue cheque books to their customers which make the business transactions quite easy. A businessman is not required to carry heavy cash along with him. He can make the payment in the form of cheques. The cheques are deposited in the bank and in turn the bank issuing the cheque book will pay the amount from the account of account holder provided the same amount is present in his account. If the amount as that of cheque issued is not present in his account then the cheque will be dishonoured and customer issuing the cheque may be punished according to law.

B. Secondary functions

In addition to the above mentioned primary functions the banks also perform other functions known as secondary functions which include agency functions and utility functions as given below :

1. The banks collect cheques, bills and interest etc. on behalf of its customers.
2. The banks pay regular instalments of insurance premium, taxes and other kind of instalments on behalf of the customers.
3. The banks collect fees on behalf of various Government and private educational institutions.
4. A bank undertakes credit transfer from one branch to another branch.
5. The banks provide lockers to the customers for keeping their valuable articles like gold jewellery, securities, shares and other important documents in the safe custody of banks. Lockers are different sized cupboards provided in the strong room of the bank. The customers can put their own lock to the locker and are free to operate at any time.
6. Money can be transferred from one part of the country to another part of the country through banks in the form of cheques or drafts.
7. The banks help those persons who are planning to go abroad by arranging foreign exchange for them.
8. The banks buy and sell shares/bonds/debentures on behalf of their customers.
9. Now a days prospects and application forms of various educational institutions and other organisations are sold and accepted by the banks.

10. The banks provide expert advice to the customers regarding the investments and other financial matters as they always deal in money transactions. Some of the banks publish the information regarding financial matters, trade and commerce in various magazines and newspapers for the benefit of their customers.

For all kinds of above mentioned services the banks charge some commission in the form of service charges without which it may not be possible for the banks to work effectively and efficiently.

From the above mentioned services and functions it is quite clear that the banks perform different kinds of important functions without which it may be extremely difficult for a society to survive and the country as a whole may not develop and progress effectively.

Financial planning

Finance is the life-blood of any business, big or small. Its necessity is felt at all levels in the business organisations. No activity in the business can be carried out without finance. For a pharmaceutical organisation finance is required for the following purposes :

1. To acquire land, building, machinery and equipment.
2. To purchase raw materials and other necessary items.
3. To pay wages, salaries and other incidental charges.
4. To pay rent, insurance, taxes and advertising charges etc.
5. To maintain a regular supply of the products in the market.
6. To allow credit to the wholesalers and other user departments.

Now a days the importance of finance has increased to a great extent as no activity can be carried out without finance and difficulties being faced in raising the finance. Therefore it has become necessary for the students of pharmacy to study and gain knowledge in financial planning.

Finance may be defined as the science and art of raising and spending money. According to Guthmann and Dougall, "Business finance can be broadly defined as the activity concerned with the planning, raising, controlling and administering the funds used in the business."

Financial management

Financial management is one of the most important functions of pharmaceutical management because the success of any company greatly depends on the acquisition and proper utilisation of financial resources. For the proper handling of finance it is necessary that the organisation should have a well-trained and experienced financial manager who will look after all the financial activities including raising of sufficient funds, budgeting, lending and borrowing policies and management of fixed and current assets. If proper financial management techniques are used the pharmaceutical companies can reduce their capital employed and improve their return on investments in men and machines.

Objectives of financial management

The financial management has the following objectives :

1. To provide continuous supply of adequate funds to the business.
2. To ensure a fair return on investment to the investors.
3. To generate and build up sufficient surplus and reserves for the growth and expansion of the organisation.
4. To co-ordinate with other departments of the organisation in the use of financial resources.
5. To plan, direct and control the utilisation of finances in the best possible manner to ensure maximum efficiency of the operations.
6. To develop and maintain proper relations with suppliers, financiers, workers and members of the organisation.

Financial planning

Financial planning may be defined as the process of deciding in advance the financial activities necessary for a pharmaceutical company to achieve its basic objectives. Once it is decided to set up an industry or shop it becomes necessary to chalk out the financial plan of the company. The most important is to determine the amount of capital which will be needed for the company at present and in future. Special thought must also be given to the frequent difficulties which may arise from time to time that may hamper the growth of the business. Financial planning also involves estimation of the amount of promotion expenses, expenses on organisation, cost of fixed assets, operating costs and cost of getting the business established. Taking into consideration these points a businessman should device the long-term financial plans for the success of the business in future also.

For the success of any pharmaceutical company, sound financial planning is very necessary which is done under the following aspects :

1. To estimate the amount of capital to be raised for the company.
2. To work out that how much of these requirements will be met by the internal sources and how much will be raised from outside sources.
3. To find out sources and develop best possible plans for obtaining funds from outside sources.
4. To determine policies for handling, collection and repayment of finances.
5. To decide that how much amount of funds is to be invested in fixed and working capital.
6. To determine the overall profits of the company and best utilisation of funds.

Characteristics or principles of financial planning

A good financial plan should have the following characteristics :

1. It should be simple so that it is easily managed and understood even by a layman.
2. It should have long foresight, that means it should not only meet the present requirements but future requirements must also be taken into

consideration. A plan prepared without foresight may prove disastrous for the company.

3. It should be flexible that the plans may be changed according to the needs.
4. It should provide maximum utilisation of funds and prevent wasteful expenditure of funds.
5. It should provide sufficient cash in hand to pay salaries, wages, cash purchases and other incidental expenses.
6. It should withstand the emergency financial difficulties which may hamper the growth of the business.
7. It should be economical that the cost of raising capital from outside sources should be minimum.

Sources of finance

The financial requirements of a business can broadly be classified into three categories :

1. Short term financial requirements.
2. Medium term financial requirements.
3. Long term financial requirements.

Short term finances are required for meeting working capital needs. They are usually required for a period up to one year and are raised from sources which can provide funds only for a short period, quickly and at reasonable cost. Such finances are raised from trade credit, bank credit, instalment credit and customer advances.

Medium term finances are required for a period of more than one year but less than ten years. They are raised from issue of preference shares, issue of debentures, public deposits, bank loans and from special industrial finance institutions.

The long-term funds are required to a great extent for meeting the fixed capital requirements of the business. They are required for a period exceeding ten years or for indefinite period. These funds are raised from those sources which provide the funds in an uninterrupted way and for a long period e.g. shares, debentures, loans from specialised institutions, commercial banks etc.

The different sources of finance are as follows :

1. Internal sources (Owned capital)
2. External sources (Borrowed capital)

1. Internal sources

(a) Issue of shares : For small scale business the businessman invests his own savings as in one man business or in partnership with other persons. But for large scale business the big organisations or companies issue ownership shares or debentures to the public.

A share may be defined as one of the units into which the share capital of a company has been divided and the person holding the share is known as shareholder. For example, the total capital of a company may consist of one crore rupees which is divided into parts or shares of Rs. 1,000 each. Each shareholder is permitted to buy specified number of shares. The profit earned by the company is divided amongst the shareholders proportional to the value of the shares held by them. The profit so divided amongst the shareholders is known as dividend. A shareholder becomes a part owner of the company and the capital so raised is known as 'owned capital' and the shares are called 'ownership securities'. The shareholders appoint directors who run the day to day affairs of the company.

Types of shares

There are two types of shares :

1. Preference shares
2. Equity shares.

1. Preference shares

Preference shares are those shares which get preference over the equity shares in the matter of distribution of dividend as well as distribution of assets in the case of winding up of the company. These shareholders get a prefixed rate of dividend which must be paid before any dividend is paid on other shares. .

2. Equity shares

Equity shares or ordinary shares are those shares which do not get any special right in the matter of distribution of dividend or in the distribution of assets in the case of winding up of the company. Equity shareholders are the real owners of the company but they get entire left out dividend only after the dividend is paid to the preference shareholders. They may not get any dividend if there is no profit. Similarly at the time of winding up of the company the equity shareholders can get the capital back only after every claim including that of preference shareholders has been settled. These shareholders have higher risk of loss of their capital if the company shows loss but at the same time they can get higher dividend if the company earns higher profits. Equity shareholders have voting right therefore they can elect directors who will look after the affairs of the company.

The capital raised from issue of shares is ideal for meeting the long-term requirements of the company because it is not to be paid back to the shareholders within the life time of the company. This capital is also used for meeting the working capital requirements of the company.

Shares can be re-purchased or re-sold in the share market, stock market or stock exchange situated at big cities like Delhi, Bombay, Calcutta, Chandigarh etc.

(b) Issue of debentures

A debenture may be defined as a document issued under the seal of the company in token of acknowledgment of debt due to the company. According to Evelyn Thomas, "Debenture is a document under the company's seal which provides for the payment of the principal sum and interest thereon at regular intervals which is usually recorded by a fixed or floating charge on the company's property or undertaking and which acknowledges a loan to the company."

The debentures are usually issued to the public in the form of bonds of Rs. 100, Rs. 200, Rs. 500, Rs. 1000 of face value. The terms and conditions for the issue of debentures are generally mentioned on the back of the debenture certificate which gives different rights to the debenture holders.

The debentures carry a fixed rate of interest which has to be paid whether the company makes any profit or not. However a debenture holder does not have any voting right and therefore cannot exercise any control over the affairs of the company. Like shares, debentures can also be re-purchased or re-sold in the share market.

(c) Ploughing back of profits or reinvestment of earning

It is a policy of certain managements that they do not distribute whole of the profit to its shareholders but retain certain amount of profit to be utilised for modernisation and expansion programmes and for meeting the fixed or working capital needs of the company. This type of financing is known as 'internal financing' or 'self financing' because the financial needs of the company are met with from internal sources.

2. External sources (Borrowed capital)

Finance can be raised from the following external sources.

(i) Debentures
(ii) Public deposits
(iii) Commercial banks
(iv) Financial institutions
(v) Trade credit

(i) Debentures

Already discussed.

(ii) Public deposits

Public deposits are the next important source of finance to that of shares and debentures. The public is asked to deposit the money in the firm for a fixed period varying from 1 to 3 years which may be renewed. The rate of interest paid is generally from 11 to 15 per cent which varies according to length of time for which the money is deposited. If a depositor so desires he can withdraw the money before the expiry of time, losing some interest.

(iii) Commercial banks

Commercial banks play an important role in supplying short-term working capital requirements of the business organisation. They make advances to the business organisations in the following forms :

(a) Loan

(b) Cash credit
(c) Hypothecation
(d) Pledge
(e) Over draft
(f) Purchasing and discounting of bills of exchange.

(iv) Financial institutions

Special financial institutions often play a vital role in the development of industries. These institutions provide medium and long-term capital, generally to the private sector organisations but sometimes to public sector undertaking also. These specialised financial institutions include :

(a) Industrial Finance Corporation of India (IFCI)
(b) Industrial Credit and Investment Corporation of India (ICICI)
(c) National Industrial Development Corporation of India (NIDCI)
(d) Industrial Development Bank of India (IDBI)
(e) State Financial Corporations
(f) State Industrial Development Corporations (SIDC)
(g) Life Insurance Corporation of India (LIC)
(h) Unit Trust of India (UTI)

(v) Trade credit

When anybody sells goods to its customers, may be manufacturer to wholesaler to retailer or to consumer, they allow credit to the buyers which they themselves get from their suppliers. This type of credit is known as trade credit. The usual duration of such credit is 30 to 90 days and no interest is charged on trade credits. It is granted to the buyers on 'open account' without any security i.e. on the goodwill and repayable capacity of the buyer.

REVISION QUESTIONS

(A) Multiple choice questions

Select the right answer and put the correct word in the respective squares given below :

1. Bank deals in :
   (a) Cash (b) Cheques/drafts
   (c) Loans (d) Deposits
   (e) All the above
2. People deposit money in banks :
   (a) For safety purposes (b) To earn interest
   (c) To deposit and withdraw money as and when required
   (d) All the above
3. Bank grant loans against :
   (a) Gold (b) National saving certification
   (c) Properties (d) All the above

4. For the services rendered by the banks they charge :
   (a) 20% as commission (b) Do not charge any commission
   (c) Nominal rate of commission (d) None of the above
5. Shareholders are the :
   (a) Managers of business (b) Owners of business
   (c) Creditors of business (d) None of the above

(B) Very short-answer type questions

Define the following :

(i) Bank (ii) Finance
(iii) Overdraft (iv) Financial management
(v) Name various Government agencies which provide loan to industrial houses

(C) Short-answer type questions

1. What do you mean by a bank? Name the facilities provided by banks.
2. Explain the primary functions of a bank.
3. What is finance? Explain what is the necessity of finance.
4. What do you understand from the term "financial management". Explain the objectives of financial management.
5. Explain short-term and medium-term financial sources.
6. Describe the long-term internal sources of finance.
7. Discuss the long-term external sources of finance.

(D) Long-answer type questions

1. Define 'bank'. Explain the functions of a bank.
2. What is finance? Why finance is necessary? Discuss various sources of finance.
3. What do you understand from the term "financial management" and "financial planning"? Discuss the objectives of financial management and principles of financial planning.
4. Write short notes on the following :
   (i) Financial management (ii) Financial planning
   (iii) Sources of finance (iv) Equity shares
   (v) Debentures (vi) Trade credit

Answers

(A)

1	2	3	4	5
e	d	d	c	b

Part II

Accountancy

Part II

Accountancy

9

Introduction to Accountancy

When a person starts any business, large or small, his main aim is to earn money. He purchases the goods at certain prices and sells them at higher prices. Thus the difference in the purchase price and sale price is his profit.

Every businessman buys and sells goods for cash as well as on credit. He receives money from persons who bought goods on credit from him and pays the money to those from whom he himself bought on credit. These purchases and sales, receipts and payments are known as business transactions.

Since every businessman does a number of transactions daily with a large number of persons, it is not possible for him to remember all the transactions therefore a proper record of these transactions is maintained which is known as book-keeping and in wider terms it is known as accountancy.

Accountancy may be defined as the language of communicating business transactions and finance information about the business. It is an art of recording the business transactions in the books of accounts in a systematic and scientific manner so as to show a true and fair picture of the business on any particular day and to keep a permanent record of business transactions.

Objects of accountancy

1. To provide knowledge of transactions.
2. To provide knowledge about creditors, debtors and overall financial positions.
3. To find out total purchases, total sales and closing stock etc.
4. To find out the net profit or loss made during a particular financial period.
5. To provide knowledge about capital assets and liabilities of the firm at any particular time.
6. To provide ready information to all interested parties.

Accounting concepts

Basic assumptions or conditions upon which the science of accounting is based is known as accounting concepts. The various accounting concepts are given below :

1. Separate entity concept
2. Dual aspect concept
3. Accounting period concept
4. Money measurement concept
5. Cost concept

6. Actual event concept
7. Going concern concept
8. Realisation concept
9. Accrual concept

1. Separate entity concept

According to this concept the business and businessman are two different entities and we have to record the transactions concerning the business and not that of businessman. Therefore even if the businessman brings something in the business or takes away anything from the business this has to be recorded in the books. Without such a distinction the affairs of the firm will be all mixed up with the private affairs of the proprietor and the true picture of the firm will not be available. Thus the concept of separate entity is applicable to all forms of business organisations i.e. proprietorship, partnership or a company.

2. Dual aspect concept

According to this concept every transaction or event has two aspects i.e. one that of debit and the other that of credit. In other words, we can say that every debit has corresponding credit and the change brought about by each transaction may be in the same direction or in the opposite direction. For example, if a concern has acquired raw materials, machinery or equipment it means the firm has given some other asset such as cash or kind.

The properties owned like land, building, machinery, furniture, raw materials and finished goods, bank cash and bills to be received by the business organisation are known as assets and the loans, bank overdrafts, creditors, bills to be paid, outstanding expenses etc. are the liabilities of the business organisation. The assets and capital of the organisation can be determined at any time from the following accounting equation :

Assets = Liabilities + Capital

Capital = Assets – Liabilities

In other words, capital i.e. owner's share is what remains to the owner when all liabilities are paid off from the available assets of the business.

A business shows income or profit if there has been an increase in the owner's share of the assets of the firm (called owner's equity) but not if the owner contributes money from himself. If the liabilities of the business are more than the assets then the business is considered in loss.

3. Accounting period concept

According to this concept a period is fixed for preparing the accounts of the business. Generally a period of 12 months is considered for which accounts are maintained. This period of 12 months is known as accounting period. A cut off date is also fixed which is generally 31st March of every year for all business purposes. Even the government has also fixed 31st March as cut off date for preparing the accounts of its departments. The last day of an accounting period is known as accounting date. At this date, the management prepares income statement i.e. profit and loss account and balance sheet to show the results of business operations within whole year. These results can be compared with the results of previous years from where the loss or gain in the particular year may be determined.

Accounting period helps in calculating the income tax to be paid, sales tax to be paid, bonus and other incentives to be given to the employees, any corrective action to be taken and future planning for the expansion of business etc. In a partnership firm and limited company all the partners and shareholders are interested in regular reports and accounts at proper intervals to know "how things are going on". This means that the final accounts must be prepared on a periodical basis rather than waiting till the business is terminated. A period of more than one year is not considered because it reduces the utility of accounting data.

4. Money measurement concept

According to this concept all the events and transactions are recorded in the books of accounts in terms of money only in whatever currency it may be and not according to items, though the quantitative records of these items are also kept but separately.

Money measurement concept is simple and easy to understand the position of the business. For example, a business enterprise has the following items :

(i) Land	2 acres
(ii) Double-storey building	
(iii) Tablet-making machines	10
(iv) Other machines	15
(v) Trucks	3
(vi) Furniture	20 Nos.
(vii) Raw material	500 kg
(viii) Cash	Rs. 20000

The above mentioned items do not convey any concrete idea about the assets the business enterprise owns but if they are expressed in terms of money and the total sum of money will give the actual position of the assets of the business enterprise as given below :

Item	In terms of money
(i) Land, 2 acres	5,00,000
(ii) Double-storey building	2,50,000
(iii) Tablet-making machines, 10	50,000
(iv) Other machines, 15	80,000
(v) Trucks, 3	5,00,000
(vi) Furniture, 20 nos.	10,000
(vii) Raw materials, 500 kg	15,000
(viii) Cash	20,000
	14,25,000

From the above table it is clear that the enterprise owns assets worth Rs. 14,25,000 (Fourteen lacs and twenty five thousands).

5. Cost concept

According to this concept all transactions are recorded at the cost price or market price whichever is less. Suppose a firm purchases a piece of land for Rs. 2 lac but the current market price is Rs. 3 lac for the same piece of land. The amount for the purchase of land will be recorded as Rs. 2 lac and not Rs. 3 lac. In the case of machinery the asset is recorded at cost at the time of its purchase but is systematically reduced in its value due to depreciation. This is one of the most important concepts as it prevents arbitrary values being put on transactions, chiefly those resulting in acquisition of assets.

6. Actual event concept

According to this concept an entry is to be recorded in books only when an event takes place. No entry should be made in the books unless and until the transaction is finalised.

7. Going concern concept

According to this concept it is assumed that the business will continue for an indefinite period and transactions are recorded from this point of view. A firm is said to be a going concern when the enterprise has neither the intention nor the necessity to wind up its affairs or decrease the scale of its operations. On the basis of this concept the outside parties will supply the goods and services and enter into long-term contracts such as giving loans, investing funds in long-term securities and giving goods on credit to the firm. But when the concern is not a going concern and is to be liquidated then all the outside parties will stop the business transactions with the gone concern. Therefore the business should go on and continue to operate at its present scale.

8. Realisation concept

According to this concept, revenue is considered as being earned on the date at which it is realised i.e. on the date when the goods are passed to the buyer either for cash or some other asset or for an agreement to pay in cash or kind. Similarly revenue from services rendered is recognised when services have been performed to the satisfaction of the customer and he has to pay for it. This can be made clear by taking the following example :

A dealer of Delhi placed an order for the purchase of goods on 15th May, 1995 to the manufacturer at Bombay. The manufacturer despatched the goods on 3rd June, 1995. The payment was received by the manufacturer on 20th June, 1995. In this case the revenue was neither realised from the date of receipt of order i.e. 15th May, 1995 nor the date of receipt of payment i.e. 20th June, 1995 but it is realised from the date of despatch of goods i.e. 3rd June, 1995.

From the above example it is clear that revenue is neither earned when an order is received nor when the payment is received but it is deemed to have been earned when the goods are actually despatched to the customer.

9. Accrual concept

Accrual concept means that all transactions or events, not yet settled in cash, must be taken into account. Similarly the cost of goods purchased must be recorded in the year in which the liabilities are incurred, regardless of when the payment is made. For example, if one borrows Rs. 50,000 at the rate of 10% p.a. At the end of the year Rs. 5,000 will become due as interest. If the amount is paid, the record will certainly show it. If, however, the amount is not yet paid, there is the liability to pay the amount which must be recorded, hence there will be no increase in assets but it will be recorded as liability.

Accrued expenses or amount yet to be paid is recorded as "accrued liability" and accrued revenues or amount to the realised is recorded as "accrued assets" in the balance sheet.

Accounting conventions

The customs or traditions which must be followed in accountancy while preparing the accounting statements are known as accounting conventions. The important accounting conventions are given below :

(i) Convention of consistency
(ii) Convention of full disclosure
(iii) Convention of conservatism

(i) Convention of consistency

According to the convention of consistency the accounting practice should remain the same from one year to another year. The comparison of the results of one accounting year with another year is possible only if the convention of consistency is strictly followed. For example, the principle of "valuing stock at cost or market price whichever is lower" should be followed every year. Similarly, if depreciation on fixed assets is provided on straight line method, it should be followed year after year to get comparable results.

It will not be proper to value stock according to one method for one year and according to another method next year. It would make the financial statement unreliable to the persons who use them. If a change becomes necessary, the change and its effects should be recorded clearly.

(ii) Convention of full disclosure

According to convention of full disclosure all the financial statements should be disclosed fully and firmly and all accounting statements should be prepared honestly. All information which is of material interest to proprietors, creditors, investors and suppliers should be disclosed clearly in the accounting statements.

(iii) Convention of conservatism

Convention of conservatism means that a gloomy picture of the business must be given due consideration. Conservatism is a policy of caution or playing safe to safeguard against possible losses of business. It takes into consideration all possible losses but do not anticipate any profits.

Book-keeping

Book-keeping is defined as the art of recording all business transactions systematically and correctly in a set of books. Book-keeping enables a person to known accurately the amount he has gained or lost in the business during a given period and to know the amount of his assets, liabilities and capital in the business on any particular date.

Book-keeping cannot be clearly distinguished from accounting. Practically both mean the same thing although the term accountancy is usually used for accounting work of a higher order. Accountancy involves the entire accounting process i.e. identification, recording, classifying and summarising in a significant manner so as to prepare accounting statements which give true picture of the business on any particular date.

Differences between book-keeping and accounting

S. No.	Book-keeping	Accounting
1.	Book-keeping is concerned with the recording of business transactions and events in a prescribed manner in the books of accounts.	Accounting is a wider term that includes book-keeping. It is primarily concerned with the design of the system of records, the preparation of reports based on the recorded data and interpretation of the reports.
2.	Book-keeper is responsible for keeping all the records of a business.	Accountants maintain the records of accounting and often direct and review the work of book-keepers.
3.	Much of the work of a book-keeper is of clerical nature which can be accomplished through the use of mechanical and electronic equipment.	The work of an accountant is of technical nature which requires much higher level of knowledge, analytical skill and patience than that required by the book-keepers.
4.	Book-keeping is more of a routine work.	Accounting is a specialised work.

Double entry book-keeping

In the modern system of book-keeping we follow the double entry system of book-keeping which essentially means that every transaction has a double aspect i.e. receiver or debtor and giver or creditor. This gives its name to the book-keeping system as "Double Entry Book-Keeping System". According to this system we have to enter every transaction twice, once on the debit side of the account which receives and again on the credit side of the account which gives. In olden days of "Bahi-Khata" only one aspect either debit or credit was used to enter which is incomplete system and not used nowadays in accountancy.

Advantages of double entry system

The double entry system has the following advantages :

1. Double entry system is a scientific system because it is based on certain principles which are applicable throughout the world.
2. Since every transaction has double aspect i.e. debit and credit aspects so it provides a systematic check on the arithmetical accuracy of the books of accounts.
3. It provides ready information regarding assets and liabilities of the company at any particular time.
4. In double entry book-keeping the chances of errors and frauds are minimised since both aspects of the transactions are to be recorded.
5. Since all the records are maintained yearly so from the books of accounts loss or gain of one year can be compared with loss or gain of another year.
6. Taking into consideration the financial position of the company the management can take the important decisions regarding business.

Disadvantages of double entry system

The double entry system has the following disadvantages :

1. According to this system a number of books of accounts are required to be maintained which is not practicable in small concerns.
2. It is a costly system because a large number of books of accounts are required to be maintained.

Terms used in accountancy

Before proceeding further with accountancy, it is very necessary to understand the terms which are commonly used in accountancy. The significant terms used are given below :

(i) Debtor

A person who receives something in cash or kind becomes a debtor.

(ii) Creditor

A person who gives something in cash or kind to another person becomes a creditor.

Supposing Sohan has taken Rs. 200 as loan (which he has to repay) from Mohan. In this transaction Sohan has received the money so he is a debtor and Mohan who has given money is the creditor. In book-keeping the debtor is represented as "Dr" and creditor as "Cr".

(iii) Business transactions

An exchange of money or money's worth as goods and services between two parties is known as business transaction.

(iv) Capital

The amount invested by the owner in the business is known as capital.

(v) Goods

Goods include all the articles or items in which a trader deals. The examples of goods include drugs, raw materials, cloth, grocery items etc.

(vi) Assets

Assets are properties owned by the businessman which has money value and can be used or sold to pay debts. The assets include land, buildings, furniture, raw materials, finished goods, machinery etc.

(vii) Liabilities

The amounts which are to be paid by the businessman to the outsiders are known as his liabilities.

(viii) Solvent

A person is said to be solvent when his assets exceed or equal his liabilities.

(ix) Insolvent

A person is said to be insolvent when his liabilities exceed his assets.

(x) Revenue

Revenue is that income which is received from the sale of goods or services rendered. It increases the capital of the businessman.

(xi) Bad debts

When the goods are sold on credit to a customer but the customer does not repay or the amount is not realised or recovered then it is known as bad debts.

(xii) Voucher

Any written document used in the business transactions is known as voucher.

(xiii) Accounts

An account is a datewise summary of all the transactions occurring in the business. The accounts may relate to a particular person, property, loss or gain e.g. bank account, Ram's account, land and building account, furniture account, wages account etc. The term account is abbreviated as 'A/c'.

Types of accounts

There are three types of accounts :

(a) Personal accounts
(b) Real accounts
(c) Nominal accounts

(a) Personal accounts

Personal accounts are those accounts which relate to individuals, group of persons, firms, associations, companies, institutions etc. For example Sohan Lal's A/c, Bharat Medical Hall A/c, Bank A/c, Lake Club's A/c, Mangat Finance Company's A/c etc.

(b) Real accounts

Real accounts are those accounts which relate to the assets of the business i.e. to the goods which can be seen, touched, purchased and sold e.g. cash A/c, land and building A/c, plant and machinery A/c, goods A/c, motor vehicles A/c etc.

(c) Nominal accounts

Nominal accounts are those accounts which relate to things which cannot be seen or touched i.e. items relating to expenses, losses, gains, incomes etc. Examples of such accounts are rent A/c, salary A/c, interest A/c, printing A/c, discount A/c, bad debts A/c, loss by fire A/c, commission A/c, etc.

Principles of accountancy

For every different account a different principle is applied. For personal A/c the principle is debit the receiver, credit the giver. For real accounts the principle is what comes in and what goes out and for nominal accounts debit all losses and expenses and credit all gains and incomes. Diagrammatically these these principles are explained as follows :

Principles of double entry

(a) Personal Accounts		(b) Real Accounts		(c) Nominal Accounts	
Debit	Credit	Debit	Credit	Debit	Credit
Receiver	Giver	What comes in	What goes out	Expenses and losses	Incomes and gains

REVISION QUESTIONS

(A) Multiple choice questions

Select the right answer and put the correct word in the respective squares given below :

1. Accounting principles are described by terms like :
   (a) Accounting concepts (b) Accounting conventions
   (c) Both (a) and (b) (d) Neither (a) nor (b)
2. Revenue is generally recognised at the point of sale. Which concept is applied in this case?
   (a) Money measurement (b) Matching
   (c) Realisation (d) Revenue realisation
3. "Each transaction has double effect" is shown by :
   (a) Cost concept (b) Dual aspect concept
   (c) Realisation concept (d) Money measurement concept
4. The transactions which cannot be recorded in terms of money are not entered in account books. The concept applied in this case is :

(a) Cost (b) Money measurement
(c) Accounting period (d) Going concern

5. Types of accounts are :
(a) Personal accounts (b) Real accounts
(c) Nominal accounts (d) Both (a) and (b)
(e) All the above

6. Which of the following is not correct :
(a) Assets = Liabilities + Capital
(b) Assets – Capital = Liabilities
(c) Assets – Liabilities = Owner's equity
(d) Assets = Capital – Liabilities

(B) Very short-answer type questions

Define the following :

(i) Accounting (ii) Accounting concepts
(iii) Accounting conventions (iv) Book-keeping
(v) Double entry book-keeping (vi) Capital
(vii) Assets (viii) Liabilities

(C) Short-answer type questions

1. What is meant by accounting principles? Briefly describe any two such principles.
2. Describe briefly what do you understand from accounting concepts and accounting conventions.
3. Enumerate various accounting conventions.
4. Write short notes on the following :
   (i) Dual aspect concepts (ii) Consistency principle
   (iii) Going concern concept (iv) Business entity concept
   (v) Money measurement concept (vi) Accrual concept
   (vii) Types of accounts (viii) Double entry book-keeping
5. Differentiate between book-keeping and accounting.

(D) Long-answer type questions

1. Define the term "Accounting". Discuss the functions of accounting.
2. What do you understand from the term "Accounting concepts"? Explain different accounting concepts used in accounting.
3. Define accounting conventions and explain different conventions used in accounting.
4. Discuss various assumptions (concepts) on which accounting is based.
5. What do you understand by double entry system? Explain its main principles and advantages of double entry system.
6. (a) Discuss different types of accounts giving suitable examples.

(b) Describe the rules for debiting and crediting for different types of accounts.

7. Describe different types of accounts and discuss the rules for debiting and crediting such accounts.

Answers

(A)

1	2	3	4	5	6
c	d	b	b	e	d

10

Cash Book

BOOKS OF ACCOUNTS

The various types of books used for recording the business transactions are known as books of accounts. These books include :

(a) Ledger—the main or principal book of accounts.

(b) Subsidiary books.

The books other than ledger used in accountancy are known as subsidiary books because they give additional help to the main book. These books are also known as books of original entry or first entry because the documents are first recorded in these books which are as follows :

(i) Journal

(ii) Cash book

(iii) Purchases day book, in which all daily purchases are recorded.

(iv) Sales day book, in which all daily sales are recorded.

(v) Purchases returns book, in which all returns (outward) of goods to the supplier are recorded.

(vi) Sales returns book, in which all returns (inward) of goods from the customers are recorded.

Cash book

The cash book is a book of accounts in which all receipts and payments of cash are recorded. The intention of preparing a cash book is to (a) separate the cash transactions from that of other accounts (b) to find out instantly the position of cash balance.

The cash book has two sides, the left hand side and the right hand side. The left hand side is the debit side in which all cash receipts are recorded and right hand side is the credit side in which all cash payments are recorded. On the debit side each item is prefixed with the word "To" and on the credit side each item is prefixed with the word "By".

An ordinary cash book is ruled as follows :

Exercise : The following transactions have taken place, make entries in the cash book.

1996			
April	1	Opening cash balance	2000.00
	4	Paid to M/s Prem Medical Hall	350.00
	5	Received from M/s A.B.C. Company	250.00
	6	Received on a/c of cash sales	200.00

Continued

An Ordinary Cash Book

Dr Cr

Date	Particulars	L.F.	Amount		Date	Particulars	L.F.	Amount	
			Rs.	P.				Rs.	P.

Continued from previous page

6	Paid to M/s Ranbaxy Pharmaceuticals	500.00
8	Paid for purchase of stationery items	30.50
9	Received on a/c of cash sales	409.50
10	Drawn for personal use	200.00
11	Paid for rent	400.00

The words c/d and b/d written on either side of the cash book stand for "carried down" and "brought down" respectively. The balance of Rs. 1379.00 written on the credit side is only to make the totals of two sides equal. The letters c/d written against the balance on credit side show that this amount will be carried down to the debit side to form the next day's opening balance and the letters b/d written on the debit side show that the amount has been brought down from the credit side. Generally the balancing of the cash book is done daily but it may be done weekly, fortnightly or monthly depending on the number of transactions made.

Types of cash books

1. Single column cash book
2. Double column cash book
3. Triple column cash book

1. Single column cash book

In this type of cash book only cash transactions in the form of notes, coins, cheques, bank drafts, postal orders are recorded. All receipts are recorded on the left hand side i.e. debit side and all payments made are recorded on the right hand side i.e. credit side. The abbreviations used are R.N. (Receipt No.) and V.N. (Voucher No.). A specimen ruling of single entry cash book is given below :

Cash Book

Dr | Cr

Date	Particulars	L.F.	Amount Rs.	Amount P.	Date	Particulars	L.F.	Amount Rs.	Amount P.
1991					1991				
April 1	To balance	—	2000	00	April 4	By M/s Prem Medical Hall		350	00
5	To M/s ABC Company		250	00	6	By M/s Ranbaxy Pharmaceuticals		500	00
6	To sales		200	00	8	By stationery A/c		30	50
9	To sales		409	50	10	By drawing A/c (for personal use)		200	00
					11	By rent A/c		400	00
								1480	50
12	To balance b/d		2859	50	11	By balance b/d		1379	00
			1379	00				2859	50

Simple Cash Book

Receipts Payments

Date	Parti-culars	R.N.	L.F.	Amount Rs.	Date	Parti-culars	V.N.	L.F.	Amount Rs.

2. Double column cash book

In this cash book apart from having the cash column we also have another column for recording discounts. The discount column on the debit sidè represents cash discount allowed and on the credit side cash discount received. Here the cash columns are balanced but discount columns are merely totalled. A specimen ruling of double column cash book is given at the following page.

3. Triple column cash book

This is the most commonly used cash book. Apart from having cash and discount columns we also have another column for bank transactions so that we can immediately know both cash in hand position and bank balance position by referring to only one account. In this book balances are worked out separately for both cash and bank columns but the discount columns are merely totalled. A specimen ruling of triple column cash book is given at the following page.

Exercise : Enter the following transactions in double column cash book.

1996		Rs.
Jan 1	Balance of cash in hand	1,600
2	Paid to Kamal Son's (discount received Rs. 45)	165
3	Cash sales	2,150
4	Purchased medicines from M/s Ranbaxy Pharmaceuticals for cash	4,500
6	Received from Chandigarh Medical Hall	1,200
8	Cash purchases of stationery items	160
9	Received from Paul Medical Hall (discount given Rs. 50)	2,500
10	Paid to Kamal Son's (discount received Rs. 80)	1,500
11	Paid to Ranbir Singh	750
12	Paid to Sohan Lal	250

Double Column Cash Book

Dr	Receipts						Payments				Cr
Date	Particulars	R.N.	L.F.	Discount Rs.	Cash Rs.	Date	Particulars	V.N.	L.F.	Discount Rs.	Cash Rs.

Triple Column Cash Book

Dr	Receipts							Payments					Cr
Date	Parti-culars	R.N.	L.F.	Discount Rs.	Cash Rs.	Bank Rs.	Date	Parti-culars	V.N.	L.F.	Discount Rs.	Cash Rs.	Bank Rs.

Solution :

Double Column Cash Book

Dr Receipts | Payments Cr

Date	Particulars	R.N.	L.F.	Discount Rs.	Cash Rs.	Date	Particulars	V.N.	L.F.	Discount Rs.	Cash Rs.
1996						1996					
Jan 1	To balance b/d				1,600	Jan 2	By Kamal Son's			45	165
3	To sales A/c				2,150	4	By purchase A/c				4,500
6	To Chandigarh Medical Hall				1,200	8	By purchase A/c				160
9	To Paul Medical Hall			50	2,500	10	By Kamal Son's			80	1,500
						11	By Ranbir Singh				750
						12	By Sohan Lal				250
						12	By balance c/d				125
				50	7,450					125	7,450
13	To balance b/d				125						

Exercise : Enter the following transactions in the triple column cash book and balance the cash book.

1996			Rs.
May	1	Opening balance (Cash in hand)	5000
		(Cash in bank)	8000
	2	Received cash from M/s Amit Son's and allowed cash discount of Rs. 100	1000
	3	Sold goods for cash	2500
	4	Paid to M/s Om Medicos by cheque	3800
	6	Paid to staff as salary by cheques	5000
	7	Received from Verma Medical Hall by cheque (allowed discount of Rs. 50)	2500
	8	Paid as rent by cheque	1500
	10	Drew from bank	1200
	11	Drew cash for personal use	1000

Balancing the cash book

When the cash book is completed, the businessman can find out the balance in hand or the amount of money he should have in his cash book. The method of calculating and recording balance in hand is called balancing the cash book. The cash book can be balanced by totalling the cash amount on either side of the cash book i.e. the debit side and the credit side and find out the difference. The total of the cash column on the debit side is always more than the cash column on the credit side, it can never be less. This is because the trader cannot pay more than he has. If the trader is to pay something out of the amount borrowed from somebody, the amount borrowed will first have to be recorded on the debit side before he pays anything to somebody which will also be recorded on the credit side. If the trader pays every pie he has then the totals of the two sides will be equal. In such a case there will be no balance.

Petty cash book

In big business establishments there are several petty and insignificant expenses like postage, carriage, cooliage, refreshment to visitors which are generally paid in cash. In order to prevent the entry of all these small expenses in cash book, a separate book called "Petty Cash Book" is used for recording these day to day expenses. Generally the petty cash book is maintained on an imprest system which means that the petty cashier is given a fixed sum of rupees in the beginning of the month and out of this amount he keeps on spending money for business purposes and also keeps on recording all these transactions. At the end of the month the balance in his hand is worked out and he is given a sum equal to what he has spent so that he again has the same balance with which he started. A specimen ruling of petty cash book is given under the heading simple petty cash book.

Solution :

Triple Column Cash Book

Dr	Receipts											Payments	Cr
Date	Particulars	R.N.	L.F.	Discount Rs.	Cash Rs.	Bank Rs.	Date	Particulars	V.N.	L.F.	Discount Rs.	Cash Rs.	Bank Rs.
1996							1996						
May 1	To balance b/d				5000	8000	May 4	By Om Medicos					3800
2	To Amit Son's			100	1000		6	By salary A/c					5000
3	To sales A/c				2500		8	By rent A/c					1500
7	To Verma Medical Hall			50		2500	11	By personal A/c				1000	
10	To bank					1200	12	By balance c/d				7500	1400
				150	8500	11700						8500	11700
14	To balance b/d				7500	1400							

Methods of writing of petty cash book

There are two methods of writing petty expenses in the petty cash book.

(i) Simple petty cash book
(ii) Analytical petty cash book

(i) Simple petty cash book

A simple petty cash book is just like a simple cash book. The amount of cash received from the cashier, cash book folio, date, particulars, V.N., L.F. and amount paid are entered in respective columns. A specimen ruling of simple petty cash book is given below :

Simple Petty Cash Book

Amount received	Cash book folio	Date	Particulars	V.N.	L.F.	Amount paid Rs.

(ii) Analytical petty cash book

A simple petty cash book is sufficient for small business but in large scale business a huge amount is spent on petty expenses of different items. From a simple petty cash book a petty cashier is not in a position to tell how the amount was spent on different petty expenses but from analytical petty cash book he can immediately tell how the money was spent on petty expenses under various heads.

The analytical petty cash book has two sides, the debit side and the credit side. The amounts received from the main cashier are entered on the left hand side i.e. the debit side and payments are entered on the right hand side i.e. the credit side of the petty cash book. On the credit side there are a number of columns to enter payments for, say, conveyance, stationery, postage and telegrams, carriage and cooliage, miscellaneous etc. The ruling of analytical petty cash book is given on the following page.

Exercise : Prepare an analytical cash book on imprest system from the following particulars. On July 1, 1996, petty cashier was having Rs. 60 in hand and had received Rs. 500 from head cashier for petty cash payments. The particulars of petty expenses during the month are as follows :

Analytical Petty Cash Book

Cash received Rs.	C.B.F. No.	Date	Particulars	V. No.	Total payment Rs.	Conveyance Rs.	Stationery Rs.	Postage and telegrams Rs.	Carriage and cartage Rs.	Printing and advertisement Rs.	Miscellaneous Rs.	Remarks

C.B.F. No. = Cash book folio number; V. No. = Voucher number

Date	Particulars	Expenditure Rs.
1996		
July 1	Paid taxi fare for Manager	100
4	Paid for telegram	10
6	Paid for postage	5
10	Paid for electric repairs	25
15	Paid for freight	55
20	Paid for stationery	15
25	Paid for printing	110
28	Refreshment for visitors	35
30	Carbon papers	15
31	Coolie charges	10
31	Paid for railway freight	60

REVISION QUESTIONS

(A) Objective type questions

Put ✓ for correct answer and ✕ for wrong answer in the respective squares given below :

1. Cash book records cash transactions only.
2. All columns of the three column cash book are balanced.
3. Machinery purchased on credit will be recorded in cash book.
4. Petty cash book is used for entering petty purchases only.
5. Petty cash book is maintained by the accountant.
6. Cash book is a subsidiary as well as principal book of accounts.
7. Opening balance will appear only in two columns of three column cash book.
8. Discount columns in the cash book are only memorandum columns; really they are not a part of the cash book.
9. The 'imprest system' is used in relation to purchases book.
10. A cash book becomes more reliable if it is balanced every day.

1	2	3	4	5	6	7	8	9	10

(B) Very short-answer type questions

Define the following :

(i) Transaction
(ii) Cash book
(iii) Petty cash book
(iv) Double column cash book
(v) Triple column cash book
(vi) Cash discount
(vii) Trade discount
(viii) Balancing the cash book

Solution :

Analytical Petty Cash Book

Cash received Rs.	C.B.F. No.	Date	Particulars	V. No.	Total payment Rs.	Conveyance Rs.	Stationery Rs.	Postage and telegrams Rs.	Carriage and cartage Rs.	Printing and advertisement Rs.	Miscellaneous Rs.	Remarks
		1996										
60		July 1	To balance b/d									
500		1	To cash									
		1	By taxi fare	1	100	100						
		4	By telegram	2	10			10				
		6	By postage	3	5			5				
		10	By electric repairs	4	25						25	
		15	By freight	5	55				55			
		20	By stationery	6	15		15					
		25	By printing	7	110					110		
		28	By refreshment	8	35						35	
		30	By carbon papers	9	15		15					
		31	By coolie charges	10	10				10			
		31	By railway freight	11	60				60			
					440	100	30	15	125	110	60	
		31	By balance c/d		120							
560					560							
120		Aug 1	To balance b/d									
440		1	To cash									

(C) Short-answer type questions

1. What is a cash book? Describe in brief various types of cash book.
2. What is meant by "subsidiary book"? Describe the objectives and advantages of subsidiary books.
3. Describe the method of posting the petty cash book.
4. Differentiate between cash discount and trade discount.
5. Write short notes on the following :
   (i) Cash book
   (ii) Petty cash book
   (iii) Purchases book
   (iv) Sales book
   (v) Imprest system

(D) Long-answer type questions

1. What is a cash book? Give a specimen of it. Describe the advantages of maintaining a cash book.
2. What do you understand by cash book? Describe its various types.
3. What is a petty cash book? Describe imprest system of petty cash book.
4. Describe 'Triple column cash book'. Give a proforma for the same.
5. What do you understand from purchases book and sales book? Describe the significance of maintaining such books. Give proformas for these books.

Answers

(A)

1	2	3	4	5	6	7	8	9	10
✓	×	×	✓	×	✓	✓	✓	×	✓

11

Journal, Ledger and Trial Balance

Journal

It is also known as daily record book. It is the primary and the initial book of records. The daily transactions which take place are first of all recorded in this book. From here they are posted to the ledger. The recording in this book is done according to the principles of book-keeping, i.e.,

1. Debit the receiver, credit the giver.
2. Debit what comes in, credit what goes out.
3. Debit all losses and expenses, credit all gains and incomes.

As soon as any transaction takes place we determine the different accounts to which the transaction relates i.e. personal, real or nominal. By using the above principles the transactions are recorded in the journal, the proforma of which is given below :

Journal of 'Mr. X'

Date	Particulars	L.F.	Debit Amount Rs.	Credit Amount Rs.

Exercise : Journalise the following transactions and give the nature of account (whether personal, real or nominal) in each case.

1996

Jan 1 Mr. Mohan started business with 1000 cash. He bought furniture for Rs. 1500 and goods for 1000

,, 2 Purchased goods on credit from Sohan Lal for Rs. 500

,, 3 Paid for carriage Rs. 50

,, 6 Purchased goods on cash payment for Rs. 2600

,, 7 Sold goods to Krishan Lal on cash for Rs. 1500

,, 8 Sold goods to Anil on credit for Rs. 1000

„ 10 Deposited cash in bank Rs. 800
„ 12 Paid rent Rs. 500

Solution :

Journal Entry

Date	Particulars	L.F.	Debit Amount Rs.	Credit Amount Rs.	Nature of account
1996					
Jan. 1	Cash A/c Dr		10000		Real
	To Mohan's capital A/c (started business with cash)			10000	Personal
	Furniture A/c Dr		1500		Real
	To cash A/c (bought furniture for cash)			1500	Personal
	Purchase A/c Dr		1000		Real
	To cash A/c (bought goods for cash)			1000	Personal
„ 2	Purchase A/c Dr		500		Real
	To Sohan Lal A/c (purchased goods on credit)			500	Personal
„ 3	Carriage A/c Dr		50		Nominal
	To cash A/c (paid carriage in cash)			50	Real
„ 6	Purchase A/c Dr		2600		Real
	To cash A/c (purchased goods in cash)			2600	Real
„ 7	Cash A/c Dr		1500		Personal
	To sales (sold goods on cash)			1500	Real
„ 8	Anil's A/c Dr		1000		Personal
	To sales (sold goods on credit)			1000	Real
„ 10	Bank A/c Dr		800		Personal
	To cash (deposited cash in bank)			800	Real
„ 12	Rent A/c Dr		500		Nominal
	To cash (By rent paid)			500	Real
	Total		19450	19450	

When large number of transactions are done daily, at the end of the day totals on both sides i.e. debit and credit sides of the journal are done which invariably should be the same.

Exercise : Journalise the following transactions in the books of M/s Prem Medical Hall.

1996

April 1 M/s Prem Medical Hall starts business with Rs. 20000. The firm opens an account with bank and deposits Rs. 18000 in the bank.

2 The firm purchased furniture for Rs. 850 and telephone for Rs. 2500. The payment was made by cheque.

3 Medicines were purchased from Ramesh Medical Hall for Rs. 5800 on credit.

4 Medicines were sold on credit to Garg Son's for Rs. 1200

6 Medicines were sold on credit to M/s Paul Medical Hall for Rs. 3000

7 Paid for office stationery Rs. 100

8 Paid advance rent for April Rs. 500

9 Received cash payment from M/s Paul Medical Hall Rs. 2500

10 Deposited Rs. 2000 in bank

12 Paid for electric bill Rs. 480

15 Received cash from Garg Son's Rs. 1000

Solution :

Journal of M/s Prem Medical Hall

Date	Particulars		L.F.	Dr Amount Rs.	Cr Amount Rs.
1996					
April 1	Cash A/c	Dr		20000	
	To capital account (started business with Rs. 20000)				20000
1	Bank A/c	Dr		18000	
	To cash account (cash deposited in bank)				18000
2	Furniture A/c	Dr		850	
	To bank account (furniture purchased for Rs. 850 against cheque)				850
2	Telephone A/c	Dr		2500	
	To bank account (telephone purchased for Rs. 2500 against cheque)				2500
3	Purchase A/c	Dr		5800	
	To Ramesh Medical Hall account (purchased medicines from Ramesh Medical Hall on credit)				5800

Continued

Date	Particulars		L.F.	Dr Amount Rs.	Cr Amount Rs.
4	Garg Son's A/c	Dr		1200	
	To sales account (sold medicines to Garg Son's on credit vide invoice No. ...)				1200
6	Paul Medical Hall A/c	Dr		3000	
	To sales account (sold medicines to M/s Paul Medical Hall vide invoice No. ...)				3000
7	Stationery A/c	Dr		100	
	To cash account (paid for stationery vide cash memo No. ...)				100
8	Rent A/c	Dr		500	
	To cash account (paid advance rent for April vide landlord's receipt No. ...)				500
9	Cash A/c	Dr		2500	
	To M/s Paul Medical Hall's account (received cash from M/s Paul Medical Hall vide receipt No. ...)				2500
10	Bank A/c	Dr		2000	
	To cash account (deposited cash in bank)				2000
12	Electricity A/c	Dr		480	
	To cash account (paid electric bill vide receipt No. ...)				480
15	Cash A/c	Dr		1000	
	To Garg Son's account (received cash from Garg Son's vide receipt No. ...)				1000
		Total		57930	57930

Advantages of journal

A journal has the following advantages :

1. It provides date-wise record of all the business transactions.
2. It provides complete information regarding business transactions at one place.
3. Since adequate information of all the business transactions are provided in the journal entries so there is no need to repeat the same in the ledger thus it saves the labour and the accountant is relieved from great mess of written details.
4. Each journal is a complete reflection of rule of double entry and the journal and ledger are cross indexed to each other in the procedure of posting.

5. Both debit and credit accounts of a transaction are recorded side by side in a journal so the chances of errors are reduced to a great extent.
6. As the transactions are recorded immediately in the journal as and when the transaction takes place so it eliminates the necessity of posting the ledger immediately after the transaction. The ledger can be posted from the journal at any convenient time. In a large business this consideration is of great importance.
7. The journal facilitate the discovery of errors.
8. Courts recognise the journal as evidence in proving or disproving claims because journal is a book of original entries whereas the ledger is only a summary of the original record. Courts do not accept unsupported ledger entries.

Discount

Discount is defined as the percentage of amount which is deducted from the full amount as an incentive to the customers. Sometimes the wholesalers give incentives to retailers so that they may make the payments promptly. Such discounts are of two types :

(i) Cash discount
(ii) Trade discount

(i) Cash discount

Cash discount is given to those customers who pay promptly. Some customers are slow in making payments as they use their money somewhere else. Such customers are offered cash discount so as to encourage them to make prompt payments. Generally 2% cash discount is given to those customers who pay promptly. If a customer has purchased goods worth Rs. 1000 he may pay only Rs. 980 i.e. Rs. 1000 minus Rs. 20 (which is 2% of Rs. 1000 as cash discount). Rs. 20 are entered in the discount column on the debit side of cash book. Discount allowed is a loss to the firm and will be debited to the profit and loss account. Though cash discount is a loss to the firm but it may be cheaper to give cash discount than to allow debts to accumulate and may suffer bad debts.

(ii) Trade discount

Generally trade discount is allowed under following circumstances :

(a) When a wholesaler supplies the goods to a retailer invoiced at retail price.
(b) When a customer buys the goods in bulk.
(c) When the catalogue prices have been reduced but the catalogue has not been reprinted.
(d) When the prices are reduced to sell surplus stock (as is done in woolen garments during the month of February/March every year).

Trade discount is quite different from cash discount. It is a reduction in the catalogue price or list price of an article, given by the manufacturer or wholesaler to the retailer to enable him to make a profit. Trade discount is also given on bulk buying e.g. if a trader buys 10 gross of a product at a time will be given a special discount of 5%. This 5% discount on the sale price will be known as trade discount, the amount of which will be deducted from the total amount in the invoice itself. Therefore the sales will stand reduced by the trade discount. Trade discount is not to be entered in any account as there is no such thing as a trade discount account.

The amount of trade discount allowed varies considerably from one trade to another trade or even on different articles in the same trade.

Exercise : Journalise the following transactions in the books of Ramesh.

1995
July 1 Ramesh started business with a capital of Rs. 30000.
„ 2 Purchased office furniture for Rs. 1540
„ 3 Purchased goods on credit from M/s Union Agencies for Rs. 1000
„ 4 Purchased office stationery for Rs. 180
„ 5 Sold goods for cash for Rs. 270
„ 7 Sold goods for cash to Prem Medical Hall for Rs. 750
„ 10 Returned defective goods to M/s Union Agencies for Rs. 100
„ 10 Paid Rs. 800 in cash to M/s Union Agencies
„ 11 Opened a saving bank account with Rs. 10000
„ 12 Returned goods by Prem Medical Hall for Rs. 100
„ 20 Paid insurance premium by cheque for Rs. 325
„ 22 Purchased electric goods for Rs. 290
„ 22 Purchased goods worth Rs. 950 and payment was made by cheque
„ 27 Cash sales for Rs. 500
„ 28 Paid rent Rs. 120
„ 30 Paid salary to chowkidar Rs. 75
„ 30 Paid water bill Rs. 35
„ 31 Cash deposited in bank Rs. 3000

Solution :

Journal Entries

Date	Particulars	L.F.	Debit Amount Rs.	Credit Amount Rs.
1995				
July 1	Cash A/c Dr		30000	
	To capital A/c (Business started by Ramesh with capital of Rs. 30000)			30000
„ 2	Furniture A/c Dr		1540	
	To cash A/c (Purchased furniture for cash)			1540

Continued

Date	Particulars	L.F.	Debit Amount Rs.	Credit Amount Rs.
„ 3	Purchase A/c Dr		1000	
	To M/s Union Agencies (Goods purchased on credit)			1000
„ 4	Stationery A/c Dr		180	
	To cash A/c (Purchased office stationery)			180
„ 5	Cash A/c Dr		270	
	To sales A/c (Sold goods for cash)			270
„ 7	M/s Prem Medical Hall Dr		750	
	To sales A/c (Sold goods for cash)			750
„ 10	M/s Union Agencies Dr		100	
	To purchases returns A/c (Returned defective goods)			100
„ 10	M/s Union Agencies Dr		800	
	To cash A/c (Paid cash)			800
„ 11	Bank A/c Dr		10000	
	To cash A/c (Opened saving bank account)			10000
„ 12	Prem Medical Hall Dr		100	
	To sales returns A/c (Goods returned)			100
„ 20	Insurance premium A/c Dr		325	
	To bank A/c (Premium paid by cheque)			325
„ 22	Electric goods A/c Dr		290	
	To cash A/c (Purchased electric goods)			290
„ 22	Purchases A/c Dr		950	
	To bank A/c (Purchased goods by cheque)			950
„ 27	Cash A/c Dr		500	
	To sales A/c (Goods sold for cash)			500
„ 28	Rent A/c Dr		120	
	To cash A/c (Paid rent)			120
„ 30	Salary A/c Dr		75	
	To cash A/c (Paid salary to chowkidar)			75
„ 30	Water bill A/c Dr		35	
	To cash A/c (Paid water bill)			35
„ 31	Bank A/c Dr		3000	
	To cash A/c (Cash deposited in bank)			3000
	Grand total			

Sub-divisions of journal (Subsidiary books)

Though journal is one of the most important books of accounts in accountancy but it is not possible to enter all kinds of transactions in journal. So to avoid labour and time some altered forms of journal known as subsidiary journals or subsidiary books are used for recording certain class of transactions. These books are also known as books of original entry or first entry because the documents are first recorded in these books. These subsidiary books are also known as 'day books' because the documents are first recorded daily in these books and then the entries are transferred to other books of accounts.

The following day books are commonly used for this purpose :

(i) Purchases day book
(ii) Sales day book
(iii) Purchases returns book
(iv) Sales returns book

(i) Purchases day book

Purchases day book is also known as invoice book, bought book or purchases journal. The goods which are bought on credit only though by post or otherwise are entered in this book. The goods bought for cash are not entered into purchases book but are entered in the cash book. The purchase of furniture, office equipment, land, building etc. which constitute assets are not entered in purchases book but are entered in general journal if purchased on credit but if purchased for cash then it is entered in cash book. When the goods are bought, along with the goods a statement giving the particulars of the goods is received which is known as invoice.

FORMS OF INVOICES (FORMAT)

Invoice

While sending goods, the seller sends to the buyer a document which is based on the settled terms. It contains complete details of the goods and the various expenses incurred in this connection. Through the medium of this document the buyer comes to know as how much amount he has to pay to the seller. This document is known as invoice in commercial language.

Format of invoice

The format of invoice is given on the following page.

On receipt of the invoice, the quantities of goods as shown in the invoice are checked and the total amount item-wise is also calculated just to see that there is no arithmetic error. After checking the quantities and amount the contents are entered in the purchases book. There is no need to record the full details in the purchases book, as the invoices themselves are carefully filed and can be consulted as and when the need arises. The trade discount and other details are not recorded in the purchases journal.

INVOICE

Telegram : Medicare

Phone No. : 24762

Paul Medicos

Invoice No. ....

Address :
S.C.F. 34, Sector 22 A
Chandigarh

Dated ....

To

M/s ....
....

Order No. ....

Despatched by ....

Dated ....

Rail/Truck Receipt No. ....

S. No.	Particulars	Qty.	Rate	Amount	
				Rs.	P.

Total amount in words ....

E. & O. E.

For Paul Medicos

Terms and conditions of payment

Sd. ....

The transactions which are properly recorded in purchases journal are then posted to the ledger. The posting of the ledger may be done daily and totaling of the purchases book may be done monthly which is then posted to the debit side of the ledger.

The format of the purchases journal is given on the following p

Purchases Journal

Date	Invoice No.	Name of the supplier	L.F.	Amount Rs.
1996				
March 1	2127	Ranbaxy Labs	2	2520.00
4	1565	Pfizer Ltd.	4	5430.00
5	560	Warner	8	3665.00
6	1872	Parke Davis	7	7742.00
7	4217	Ranbaxy Labs	2	3645.00
				23,002.00

Exercise : From the following transactions, prepare the purchases book of M/s Bharat Medicos and post them in ledger.

Date	Invoice No.	Particulars	Amount Rs.
1996			
July 5	41	Purchased on credit from Naveen Chemists and Druggists	2035.00
6	10	Purchased on credit from Sahib Singh and Sons	1745.00
8	15	Purchased on credit from Dhir Bros.	1832.00
9	12	Purchased for cash from M/s Prem Medical Hall	752.00
11	9	Purchased office furniture on credit from Popular Furnitures	2517.00

Solution :

Purchases book of M/s Bharat Medicos

Date	Invoice No.	Name of supplier	L.F.	Amount Rs.
1996				
July 5	41	Naveen Chemists and Druggists		2035.00
6	10	Sahib Singh & Sons		1745.00
8	15	Dhir Bros.		1832.00
		Total		5612.00

Note : The cash purchases from M/s Prem Medical Hall on July 9 is not entered in the purchases book but it is recorded in the cash book. Similarly the purchase of office furniture on July 11 from Popular Furnitures is not entered in the purchases book but it is entered in the journal.

Ledger account

Purchases account

Date	Particulars	J.F.	Amount Rs.	Date	Particulars	J.F.	Amount Rs.
1996 July 31	To purchases as per purchase book		5612.00				

Naveen Chemists and Druggists

				1996 July 5	By purchases		2035.00

Sahib Singh & Sons

				1996 July 6	By purchases		1745.00

Dhir Bros.

				1996 July 8	By purchases		1832.00

(ii) Sales day book

Sales day book is also known as sales book or sales journal. The goods which are sold on credit only are entered in the sales book. The goods which are sold for cash are recorded in the cash book. The things other than goods sold on credit are not entered in sales book but are entered in the journal.

The entries in the sales book are recorded from the sales invoices or bills issued by the firm to the customers. The total of the sales book shows the total credit sale of goods during the concerned period. Usually, the sales book is totalled every month.

The transactions recorded in the sales book are then posted to the ledger. A separate account will have to be opened in the ledger for each customer whom the goods have been sold on credit and will be debited with the amount of each sale. At the end of the month, the credit sales would be added, and the totals thus obtained would be credited to goods account. The double entry of the sales book would thus be completed.

The format and preparation of the sales journal is given below :

Sales Journal

Date	Invoice No.	Name of customer	L.F.	Amount Rs.
1996				
July 1	121	M/s Raman Kumar & Sons, Amritsar	25	632.00
2	122	Mr. Pardeep Jain, Delhi	20	1575.00
3	123	M/s Allwell Chemists, Delhi	22	878.00
4	124	M/s Prem Medical Hall, Chandigarh	15	2105.00
5	125	Mr. Pardeep Jain, Delhi	20	747.00
				5937.00

Exercise : From the following transactions prepare the sales book of M/s Prem Medical Hall, wholesale chemist and post them in ledger.

Date	Invoice No.	Particulars	Amount Rs.
June 2	15	Sold on credit to M/s Sudhir Medicos	532.00
4	16	Sold for cash to Rama Stores	1050.00
6	17	Sold on credit to Chandigarh Medical Hall	945.00
7	18	Sold on credit to Verma Medicos	527.00
8	19	Sold for cash to Prem Bros.	1230.00

Solution :

Sales book of M/s Prem Medical Hall

Date	Invoice No.	Name of customer	L.F.	Amount Rs.
June 2	15	M/s Sudhir Medicos	7	532.00
6	17	Chandigarh Medical Hall	9	945.00
7	18	Verma Medicos	15	527.00
		Total		2004.00

Note : Cash sale to Rama Stores on June 4 and cash sale to Prem Bros. on

June 8 are not entered in sales book but both these transactions must be entered in the cash book.

Ledger account

Sales account

Dr							Cr
Date	Particulars	J.F.	Amount Rs.	Date	Particulars	J.F.	Amount Rs.
				June 30	By sales as per sales book		2004.00

M/s Sudhir Medicos

June 2	To sales		532.00				

Chandigarh Medical Hall

June 6	To sales		945.00				

Verma Medicos

June 7	To sales		527.00				

(iii) Purchases returns book

It generally happens in actual business that a trader, in his capacity as a purchaser at certain occasions may have to return the goods to the seller from whom he himself has bought the goods. The goods may have to be returned due to the reason that :

(a) the goods are not up to the required standards or specifications;

(b) some other goods have been sent by error;

(c) due to some defects.

If the goods are returned now and then, it may be entered in the journal itself but if the return of goods is too frequent then a separate book should be used to record the return of goods. The name of the book in which the return of goods is entered is known as purchases returns book, returns outward book or purchases returns journal.

When the goods purchased are returned to the supplier due to any reason, a debit note is prepared in duplicate, one copy of which is sent to the supplier and the other copy is retained in the office for office record. A debit note contains serial No., date, name of the party to whom the goods have been returned, details of goods returned and reason for returning the goods. The amount of debit note is posted immediately in the suppliers account. At the end of the month total of the purchases returns are done which are then credited to the purchases return account.

The format and preparation of the debit note and the purchases returns book is given below :

Debit Note

Paul Medical Hall
Chandigarh

Chandigarh
3.11.95

M/s Pardeep and Co.,
Delhi

Particulars	Amount Rs.
To goods returned	
10 pkts Avil ampoules	200
5 × 100 cap Ampicillin	1000
50 bottles Normal saline	750
Total	1950

E. & O. E. For Paul Medical Hall

Partner

E. & O. E. stands for errors and omissions excepted means clerical errors can be rectified later on.

If there is an error in the bill and the customers are to be charged more say the price charged is less than the right one, then the debit notes are also prepared and sent to them. In fact, the invoice made for the customer is a debit note.

Purchase returns book

Date	Debit Note No.	Name of supplier	L.F.	Amount Rs.
1996				
Aug. 12	51	M/s Sodhi Medical Hall		1545.00
18	52	Kuldeep & Co.		936.00
25	53	Allwell Chemists		1232.00
30	54	Singh Bros.		765.00
				4478.00

(iv) Sales returns book

The goods sold on credit can be returned by the customer to the seller due to defective items, items not ordered or due to any other reason. If the number of returns are only a few, it may be entered in the journal but if the return of goods is too frequent then a separate book should be used to record the return of goods. The name of the book in which the return of goods is entered is known as the sales returns book, returns inward book or sales return journals.

When the goods sold are received back from the customer, a credit note is prepared in duplicate, one copy of which is sent to the customer who has returned the goods and the other copy is retained by the seller for office record. The credit note contains serial No., date, name of customer who has returned the goods, detail of goods returned and reason for returning the goods. The individual amounts of credit note are posted immediately in the customer's account. At the end of the month total of the sales returns are done which are then debited to the sales returns account.

The format and preparation of the credit note is given on the following page and the sales returns book is given below :

A credit note is usually printed in red ink.

Date	Credit Note No.	Name of customer	L.F.	Amount Rs.
1996				
July 10	10	Rama Son's, Ludhiana		560.00
15	11	Krishan Bros., Delhi		1825.00
28	12	Panchvati Medicos, Rohtak		1275.00
30	13	Bahl Son's, Rurki		638.00
				4298.00

Credit Note

Pardeep & Co.
Delhi

Delhi
3.7.1996

Paul Medical Hall
Chandigarh

Particulars	Amount Rs.
By goods returned	
10 pkts Avil ampoules	200
5 × 100 cap Ampicillin	1000
50 bottles Normal saline	750
Total	1950
E. & O. E. For Pardeep & Co.	
Partner	

Ledger

Ledger is the principal or chief book of accounts because all the transactions recorded in the journal or other subsidiary books will have to be posted in the ledger. In a ledger individual record of every different account is maintained in a very systematic manner from where the businessman can find out the balance of that particular account at any time. Ledger contains all accounts whether personal, real or nominal.

Ledger is a register or bound book. It contains a number of pages known as Ledger Folio (L.F.). These pages are numbered consecutively. Usually one account is entered at one page and if number of transactions are more, it may be carried to more than one page. An index is made at the beginning of the ledger for easy reference.

The proforma of ledger is as follows :

Name of Account

Dr Cr

Date	Particulars	J.F.	Amount Rs.	Date	Particulars	J.F.	Amount Rs.

Point to be noted

While posting the ledger the following points must be noted :

1. All the transactions are entered in the ledger accounts in order of dates.
2. Every entry must be dated and date entered in the respective columns.
3. A ledger account is divided into two sections by a central vertical line. The left hand side is known as debit side and the right hand side is known as credit side. The debit side is represented by 'Dr' and credit side by 'Cr' which are written on the left hand and right hand corners respectively.
4. Every entry on the debit side (left hand side) of the account commences with the word "To".
5. Every entry on the credit side (right hand side) of the account commences with the word "By".
6. In the folio column of the ledger account the page No. of journal from where the entries are posted in the ledger are entered. Similarly, in the folio column of the journal, the page No. of ledger account to which the entry is posted is entered.

Importance of ledger

A ledger is the principal or chief book of accounts. It is very important and useful for a business organisation because :

1. At a glance, the businessman can find out at once that what amount is due to certain customer to whom the goods were sold on credit and what amount he has to pay to the dealers from whom he himself bought the goods on credit.
2. In the ledger individual record of every different account is maintained in a very systematic manner from where the businessman can find out the balance of that particular account at any time.
3. In a journal various transactions pertaining to an account may be entered at different pages but in a ledger such transactions are entered on one page in the ledger.

4. The account of any particular person or firm can be easily located in a ledger by going through the index made at the beginning of the ledger.
5. By consulting the ledger the businessman can immediately come to know whether he has made a profit or has suffered losses. If so, how much profit or loss. He can also come to know that what was his capital position on any particular date.

Difference between Journal and Ledger

S. No.	Journal	Ledger
1.	It is a book of original entry or subsidiary book.	It is the principal book of accounts or book of second (or final) entry.
2.	It is a book of chronological record i.e. day to day transactions are recorded as and when they take place.	It is a book of analytical record of all the transactions entered in the journal.
3.	In journal balancing is not done.	In ledger all the accounts are balanced.
4.	From the journal, the entries are transferred to the ledger.	From the ledger, the trial balance is prepared and then from here financial statements are prepared.
5.	The process of making entries in the journal is known as journalising.	The process of making entries in the ledger is known as posting.
6.	The ruling of journal has one column for particulars and two columns for amount, one for debit amount and the other for credit amount.	The ruling of ledger is equally divided into two sides. The left hand side is known as the debit side and the right hand side is known as the credit side.

Ledger posting of journal

Every transaction is first recorded in journal and from the journal it is transferred to the concerned accounts in ledger. This process of transferring the entries from the journal to the ledger is known as 'posting'. Every journal entry involves at least two accounts, indicating the accounts to be debited or credited. The actual work of debiting and crediting is done in the ledger. While posting from the journal, the Dr account is debited and the Cr account is credited.

Exercise : From the following journal entry at J.F. 15 prepare a ledger.

Date	Particulars	L.F.	Dr Amount Rs.	Cr Amount Rs.
1996				
Jan 1	Cash A/c Dr		10000	
	To Raman's capital A/c (For starting business with cash)			10000

Solution :

Cash Account

15

Dr Cr

Date	Particulars	L.F.	Amount Rs.	Date	Particulars	L.F.	Amount Rs.
1996 Jan 1	To capital	18	10000				

Capital Account

18

Date	Particulars	L.F.	Amount Rs.	Date	Particulars	L.F.	Amount Rs.
1996				Jan 1	By cash A/c	15	10000

Exercise : From the following transactions, make journal entries and post them in ledger. March 31 rent Rs. 800, wages Rs. 500 and salaries Rs. 1200 paid in cash.

Solution :

Journal Entry

Date	Particulars		L.F.	Dr Amount Rs.	Cr Amount Rs.
Mar. 31	Rent A/c	Dr		800	
	Wages A/c	Dr		500	
	Salaries A/c	Dr		1200	
	To cash A/c (Rent, wages and salaries paid in cash)				2500

Solution :

Ledger Posting

Rent Account

Dr Cr

Date	Particulars	J.F.	Amount Rs.	Date	Particulars	J.F.	Amount Rs.
Mar 31	To cash A/c		800				

Wages Account

Dr Cr

Date	Particulars	J.F.	Amount	Date	Particulars	J.F.	Amount
Mar 31	To cash A/c		500				

Salaries Account

Dr Cr

Date	Particulars	J.F.	Amount	Date	Particulars	J.F.	Amount
Mar 31	To cash A/c		1200				

Cash Account

Dr Cr

Date	Particulars	J.F.	Amount	Date	Particulars	J.F.	Amount
				Mar 31	By rent A/c		800
					By wages A/c		500
					By salaries A/c		1200

Exercise : From the following transactions, prepare journal and post the entries into ledger.

1996		
Sept 1	Cash sales to Ram Kumar & Sons	6000
4	Goods purchased from Devi Parshad on credit	2800
8	Rs. 2700 paid in cash to Devi Parshad who allowed Rs. 100 as cash discount	

Solution :

Journal

35

Date	Particulars	L.F.	Dr Amount Rs.	Cr Amount Rs.
1996				
Sept 1	Cash A/c Dr		6000	
	To sales account (Goods sold on cash basis)			6000
4	Purchase A/c Dr		2800	
	To Devi Parshad (Goods purchased from Devi Parshad on credit)			2800
8	Devi Parshad			
	To cash account			2700
	To discount account (Cash paid to Devi Parshad and discount allowed by him)			100

Ledger posting

Cash Account

Dr Cr

Date	Particulars	J.F.	Amount Rs.	Date	Particulars	J.F.	Amount Rs.
1996							
Sept 1	To sales account	35	6000	Sept 8	By Devi Parshad	35	2700

Sales Account

				Sept 1	By cash account	35	6000

Purchases Account

Sept 4	To Devi Parshad	35	2800				

Discount Account

				Sept 8	By Devi Parshad	35	100

Devi Parshad's Account

Sept 8	To cash account	35	2700		By purchases account	35	2800
	To discount account	35	100				

Trial balance

We have learnt that the fundamental principle of double entry is that for every debit there must be a corresponding credit. Thus for every debit or a number of debits, to one or more accounts there must be a corresponding credit or credits of the same amount. Thus it follows, that the sums of the debit amount must be equal to the sums of the credit amounts of the ledger at any date. Just to check whether the entries are correct or not, a statement is prepared known as trial balance.

After preparing the journal and posting the entries in a ledger, the balances are worked out. These balances of all the accounts are carried to a separate sheet of loose paper. The debit balances and credit balances of each and every account are entered in respective columns. Then the sums of debit balances and credit balances is worked out which should be equal on both sides which signifies that the accounts have been properly posted and the balances have been correctly worked out. However, if they do not tally, it means some mistake has been done while posting the journal entry into the ledgers which requires checking and correction.

Therefore trial balance is very important statement just to see that the accounts have been properly compiled and arithmetically correct.

Objects of preparing a trial balance

1. The balance of any account at any time can be found in the trial balance at a glance.
2. With trial balance it can be found out whether the accounts are being maintained properly and the transactions are correctly recorded or not.
3. It helps in the preparation of trading account, profit and loss account and balance sheet because the balances of all the accounts are entered at one place.

Methods of preparing trial balance

The trial balance can be prepared by using any one of the following methods :

(i) Total method

(ii) Balance method

(i) Total method

According to this system the totals of debit side and credit side of each ledger account is recorded under the debit side and credit side of the trial balance. Then the grand total of debit side as well as credit side are done. If these totals tally with each other, it means the books of account are arithmetically correct but if there is difference in grand totals it means there is some mistake in the accounts which must be rechecked.

(ii) Balance method

According to this method all the ledger accounts are first balanced immediately after posting the ledger from the books of original entry to the ledger. The balance of debit and credit side of each account is then transferred to the trial balance account and totalled. Accounts having no balance is not transferred to the trial balance. If the grand totals of both the sides i.e. debit side and credit side tally with each other it means the books of account are arithmetically correct but if there is difference in grand totals it means there is some mistake in the accounts which must be rechecked. This method is generally used in practice as it makes the calculation easy and facilitates the preparation of final statements of accounts.

The trial balance is prepared on a loose sheet of paper having four columns. The first column has the serial number, second name of account, third and fourth columns shows the amount of debit balance and credit balance respectively. A specimen proforma of trial balance is given below :

Trial balance as on ...

S. No.	Name of account	Dr balance (or total) Rs.	Cr balance (or total) Rs.

Trial balance of M/s Vikram Son's as on 31st March, 1995 is given below :

Trial balance as on 31st March, 1995

S. No.	Name of account	Dr Total Rs.	Cr Total Rs.
1.	Cash account	15000	7200
2.	Capital account	—	10000
3.	Goods account	6000	4500
4.	Anupam's account	3200	2700
5.	Sohan's account	1500	2500
6.	Salaries account	1000	—
7.	Rent account	200	—
		26900	26900

Sometimes a trial balance does not tally due to certain mistakes which should be rectified to tally the balances. The following are the common mistakes :

1. An item from a journal or subsidiary book may not have been posted to the ledger at all.
2. An item may have been posted in the wrong columns.
3. Wrong figures may have been entered.
4. The balance of an account may have been omitted or wrongly entered.
5. There may have been mistake in the totals of the ledger accounts.
6. A mistake may have occurred during summing the figures in the trial balance.

Exercise : From the following ledger accounts prepare a trial balance by both the methods i.e. total method and balance method.

Cash Account

Dr | | | | | | | Cr

Date	Particulars	J.F.	Amount Rs.	Date	Particulars	J.F.	Amount Rs.
1996				1996			
Jan 1	To cash A/c		10,000	Jan 5	By goods A/c		3,000
7	To goods A/c		1,000	10	By Anil		1,000
12	To Raman		2,000	15	By rent A/c		200
				31	By salaries A/c		1,000
				31	By balance c/d		7,800
			13,000				13,000
Feb 1	To balance b/d		7,800				

Capital Account

Date	Particulars	J.F.	Amount Rs.	Date	Particulars	J.F.	Amount Rs.
1996				1996			
Jan 31	To balance c/d		10,000	Jan 1	By cash A/c		10,000
				Feb 1	By balance b/d		10,000

Goods Account

Date	Particulars	J.F.	Amount Rs.	Date	Particulars	J.F.	Amount Rs.
1996				1996			
Jan 1	To cash A/c		3,000	Jan 5	By Raman		3,000
16	To Anil		2,000	7	By cash A/c		1,000
31	To Raman		500	31	By balance c/d		1,500
			5,500				5,500
Feb 1	To balance b/d		1,500				

Raman's Account

Date	Particulars	J.F.	Amount	Date	Particulars	J.F.	Amount
1996				1996			
Jan 5	To goods A/c		3,000	Jan 12	By cash A/c		2,000
				31	By goods A/c		500
				31	By balance c/d		500
			3,000				3,000
Feb 1	To balance b/d		500				

Anil's Account

Date	Particulars	J.F.	Amount	Date	Particulars	J.F.	Amount
1996				1996			
Jan 10	To cash		1,000	Jan 31	By goods A/c		2,000
Jan 31	To balance c/d		1,000				
			2,000				2,000
				Feb 1	By balance b/d		1,000

Rent Account

Date	Particulars	J.F.	Amount	Date	Particulars	J.F.	Amount
1996				1996			
Jan 15	To cash A/c		200	Jan 31	By balance c/d		200
Feb 1	To balance b/d		200				

Salaries Account

Date	Particulars	J.F.	Amount	Date	Particulars	J.F.	Amount
1996				1996			
Jan 31	To cash A/c		1,000	Jan 31	By balance c/d		1,000
Feb 1	To balance b/d		1,000				

Trial balance as on 31st January, 1996 (Total method)

S. No.	Name of account	Dr Total Rs.	Cr Total Rs.
1.	Cash account	13000	5200
2.	Capital account	—	10000
3.	Goods account	5500	4000
4.	Raman's account	3000	2500
5.	Anil's account	1000	2000
6.	Rent account	200	—
7.	Salaries account	1000	—
		23700	23700

Trial balance as on 31st January, 1996 (Balance method)

S. No.	Name of account	Dr Total Rs.	Cr Total Rs.
1.	Cash account	7800	—
2.	Capital account	—	10000
3.	Goods account	1500	—
4.	Raman's account	500	—
5.	Anil's account	—	1000
6.	Rent account	200	—
7.	Salaries account	1000	—
		11000	11000

ERRORS AND THEIR RECTIFICATIONS

Error

In every business a number of transactions are done daily and records of all these transactions are maintained. In double entry system the transactions are first entered in various subsidiary books and,then they are posted in the ledger. From the ledger the accountant prepares the trial balance, trading account, profit and loss account and lastly the balance sheet.

While preparing the above mentioned accounts an accountant can commit a number of mistakes. Such mistakes are located when we prepare the trial balance because in the trial balance the balance of the debit side and credit side does not tally but there are certain errors which do not affect the trial balance but they affect the profit and loss account and balance sheet. When an error is noticed then the accountant should use his skills to locate all the errors so that correct picture of profit and loss account is presented to the management.

The main purpose of preparing a trial balance is to test the arithmetical accuracy of the books of accounts. When totals of the trial balance are in agreement with each other then it is generally assumed that the books have been written up correctly. However, it must be kept in mind that tallying of the trial balance does not mean that no errors have been committed in the accounting records. It must be remembered that the trial balance serves to prove only the arithmetic accuracy of the books.

Errors not disclosed by trial balance

There are certain errors which remain undetected but do not affect the agreement of the trial balance. Such errors are described below :

1. Errors of omission.
2. Wrong entries in the subsidiary books.
3. Errors of principle.
4. Compensating errors.
5. Posting to wrong heads of accounts.

1. Errors of omission

An error of omission is that error where a transaction has been absolutely omitted to be recorded e.g. a credit sale of Rs. 250 to Mr. X may not have been posted to Mr. X's account in the ledger from the sales book. The result of this error will be that the debit and credit of that transaction would be omitted and the agreement of the trial balance will not be affected in any way.

2. Wrong entries in the subsidiary books

This occurs where a transaction has been wrongly entered in the subsidiary book. For example a credit sale of Rs. 540 may have been entered in the sales day book as Rs. 450.

3. Errors of principle

An error of principle is that error where a transaction is recorded against the fundamental principles of double entry. For example Rs. 9500 spent on extension of building wrongly debited to repairs account instead of building account. Such errors arise whenever an asset is treated as an expense or vice versa or a liability is treated as an income or vice versa.

4. Compensating errors

Compensating errors are those errors which cancel out one another and thus enable the trial balance to agree. For example an amount of Rs. 40 instead of Rs.

400 is debited to Anil's account and Rs. 400 instead of 40 is debited to Paul's account. Although there is an error in posting the accounts of different parties but it will not affect the trial balance because one error is compensated by another one.

5. Posting to wrong heads of accounts

Such errors arise when an amount is wrongly posted to one account instead of another account though with correct amount and on correct side. For example if a sale of Rs. 450 to M/s Paul Distributors is wrongly debited to the account of M/s Paul & Co. Since the amount entered in both the accounts is same so it will not affect the trial balance though a wrong entry has been made.

Errors disclosed by trial balance

There are a number of errors which if committed will lead to disagreement of trial balance. These errors are described below :

1. Wrong totalling or casting of the subsidiary books.
2. Posting a wrong amount to a ledger account.
3. Posting an amount on the wrong side of a ledger account.
4. Omission of an amount from ledger account.
5. Errors in balancing any ledger account.
6. An item in the subsidiary book posted twice to a ledger account.
7. An error in totalling of the trial balance will lead to disagreement of the trial balance.

Steps to locate errors

When the trial balance does not agree then the following steps should be taken to locate the errors :

1. Recheck the totals of Dr and Cr columns of the trial balance.
2. Check that the balances of all accounts including the cash and bank balances have been included in the trial balance.
3. Recheck the totals of subsidiary books specially if the error is of Rs. 1, 10, 100 and so on.
4. Check that the opening balances have been correctly brought forward in the current year's book.
5. Divide the difference of the trial balance by two and find out if any balance of the same amount is entered in the trial balance. It may have happened that such a balance might have been entered on the wrong side of the trial balance, thus causing a difference of double the amount.
6. If the difference is a large one, compare the figures of trial balance of the current year with the figures of trial balance of the previous year. If the difference between the figures of current year and previous year is large then this year's sales account should be checked again.
7. If the above mentioned steps fail to locate the errors, then check the work as follows :

   (i) Check all the totals of subsidiary books thoroughly.

(ii) Check that the totals have been brought forward carefully.
(iii) Check the postings made from journal to the ledger.
(iv) Re-check the balances extracted from the ledger.
(v) Re-check the list of balances.

If the error still remains undetected then all the subsidiary books must be cast and if necessary the posting of the ledger from subsidiary books should be rechecked.

REVISION QUESTIONS

(A) Objective type questions

Put ✓ for correct answer and ✕ for wrong answer in the respective squares given below :

1. Recording of transactions in the journal is called 'Posting'.
2. Recording of transactions in the ledger is known as 'Posting'.
3. A journal has four columns including date.
4. Ledger is the principal book of accounts.
5. In a ledger all accounts are entered in one and the same proforma.
6. The preparation of trial balance helps in locating errors of commission.
7. Writing an amount in the wrong account but on the correct side will not affect a trial balance.
8. In the journal, transactions are recorded account-wise.
9. Balance of cash account in a ledger shows cash in hand.
10. "Balance c/d" at the time of balancing the account in a ledger is written on shorter side of the account.

1	2	3	4	5	6	7	8	9	10

(B) Short-answer type questions

1. What is journal? Describe advantages of a journal.
2. What do you understand by ledger? Discuss advantages of maintaining a ledger.
3. Explain the difference between journal and ledger.
4. Write short notes on the following :
   (i) Journal (ii) Ledger
   (iii) Posting the ledger (iv) Trial balance

(C) Long-answer type questions

1. What is a journal? Explain advantages of journal and give a proforma of journal.
2. What is ledger? Why is it called the principal book of accounts? Describe the method of posting the journal into ledger.

3. Define the term "trial balance". What are the advantages of preparing trial balance?
4. What is 'trial balance'? Discuss the errors disclosed by trial balance.
5. If the debit side and credit side of a trial balance agree in amount, is this a conclusive proof of the accuracy of ledger accounts? If not, what are the errors which remain undetected in the trial balance.

Answers

(A)

1	2	3	4	5	6	7	8	9	10
×	✓	×	✓	×	✓	✓	×	✓	✓

12

Financial Statements
(Trading Account, Profit and Loss Account and Balance Sheet)

One of the main objects of maintaining accounts is to find out the profit or loss made by the business at the end of regular intervals and to ascertain the financial position of the business on a given date. These objects can be achieved by preparing final accounts at the end of each accounting period usually a year. These are known as final accounts as they are prepared at the end of the accounting period. In final accounts the financial statements are prepared. The preparation of financial statements is the last process of accounting which gives the complete information about the business.

The financial statements include two types of statements namely :

(a) profit and loss account (or income statement); and

(b) balance sheet (or position statement).

These two statements collectively are known as final accounts in accounting language.

The profit and loss account is divided into two parts :

1. Trading account
2. Profit and loss account

Trading account is not an independent account but a part of profit and loss account.

Advantages of financial statements

The financial statements provide advantages to management, creditors, shareholders and employees unions as discussed below :

1. Management

From the financial statements the management can review up-to-date progress made by the enterprise. From this progress the management can decide the future plan of action for the enterprise.

2. Creditors

From the financial statements the creditors can decide whether to expand, maintain or restrict the credit facilities to the enterprise.

3. Shareholders

From the financial statements the shareholders can gauge (judge) the financial position of the company on the basis of which they can decide whether to sell or continue their shares in the firm.

4. Employees unions

From the financial statements the employees unions can find out whether the firm is in profit or loss from where they can decide whether the firm will be in a position to enhance their wages, bonus, and other facilities or not.

Trading account

It is a part of the final accounts of the business and is prepared at the end of the financial period to determine the gross profit or gross loss of the business. It has two sides viz. the debit side and the credit side. On debit side is posted the opening stock of goods in hand, the net purchases made during the year, goods returned by the customers and the entire direct expenses like carriage incurred, wages, octroi duty etc. and on the credit side is posted the net sales, goods returned to suppliers and closing stock of goods in hand. The balancing figures of two sides, show the gross profit if the credit side is bigger and gross loss if the debit side is bigger. The sample proforma of the trading account is given below :

Trading account for the year ending 31-12-1995

Dr Cr

Particulars	Amount Rs.	Particulars	Amount Rs.
To opening stock	10000	By sales	50000
To purchases	20000	By closing stock	7500
To carriage	300	By goods (returned to supplier)	500
To wages	700		
	41000		
To gross profit	17000		
	58000		58000

Objectives of trading account

Trading account has the following objectives :

1. It provides information about the gross profit or gross loss of the company.
2. From trading account the percentage of gross profit to sales (known as gross profit ratio) can be calculated to know the success of trading.
3. Gross profit ratio of one year can be compared with the gross profit ratio of the previous year to know whether the company has made any improvement or not.
4. It helps in the calculation of ratio of cost of goods sold to sales which ultimately helps in the fixation of prices of goods of the company.

Profit and loss account

This account is prepared after the gross profit or gross loss has been ascertained by preparing the trading account. Profit and loss account is prepared in order to find out the net profit or net loss made by the firm during a particular period, which is generally one year.

Like the trading account, profit and loss account also has two sides i.e. the debit side and the credit side. On the debit side the incidental expenses for carrying out business such as salaries, rent paid, printing and stationery, advertisement etc. are entered which relate to the current year and on the credit side all incomes and gains such as rent, commission, discount or any other gain during the current year is entered. The difference between the two sides of the profit and loss account shows the net profit or net loss. The resultant balancing figure is net profit if the credit side is bigger and the net loss if the debit side is bigger. A specimen of profit and loss account is given below :

Exercise : From the information given below prepare a profit and loss account of M/s Prem Medicos for the year ending 31st December, 1995.

Gross profit	8000
Salaries	5000
Travelling expenses	500
Interest received	350
Stationery	500
Discount received	200
Advertisement	450
Rent of shop sublet	100
Office rent	300
Commission received	50
Discount allowed	250

Solution :

Profit and loss account of M/s Prem Medicos for the year ending 31st December, 1995

Dr Cr

Particulars	Amount Rs.	Particulars	Amount Rs.
To salaries	5000	By gross profit b/d	8000
To travelling expenses	500	By interest received	350
To stationery	500	By discount received	200
To advertisement	450	By rent of shop sublet	100
To office rent	300	By commission received	50
To discount allowed	250		
	7000		
To net profit	1700		
	8700		8700

Objectives of profit and loss account

The preparation of profit and loss account has the following objectives :

1. It provides information about net profit or net loss in the business during the accounting period.
2. It helps in comparing the net profit or net loss of the current year with the net profit or net loss of the previous year. From this comparison the businessman can come to know whether the performance of the business over the years is improving or declining.
3. It guides in controlling the expenses incurred on various items to improve future profitability.

Important points in profit and loss account

As the proforma of profit and loss account has two sides i.e. debit side and credit side, so the items must be entered in the respective debit and credit columns.

1. Items to be shown on the debit side of profit and loss account

The first item to be shown on the debit side of the profit and loss account is the amount of gross loss brought down from trading account. The other items of indirect expenses which are incurred to look after the business are to be included in the debit side of profit and loss account are given below :

(a) Administrative expenses

Administrative expenses are those expenses which are incurred to run the affairs of the business. These expenses include :

(i) Office salaries and wages
(ii) Rent
(iii) Printing and stationery
(iv) Postage and telegrams
(v) Telephone
(vi) Office lighting, heating and cooling
(vii) Repairs
(viii) Insurance
(ix) Accountancy fee
(x) Legal fees
(xi) Audit fees
(xii) Bank charges
(xiii) Bank commission
(xiv) Interest paid on loans
(xv) Interest on capital

(b) Selling expenses

Selling expenses include :

(i) Salesmen's salaries
(ii) Travelling expenses

(iii) Advertising
(iv) Discount allowed
(v) Bad debits
(vi) Selling commission
(vii) Brokerage
(viii) Free samples
(ix) Trade expenses
(x) Sales tax

(c) Distribution expenses

Distribution expenses are the expenses which are incurred to send the goods to the place of final distribution. These expenses include :

(i) Godown expenses
(ii) Godown insurance
(iii) Godown rent
(iv) Packing expenses
(v) Lighting of showroom and godown
(vi) Delivery van expenses

(d) Repair and depreciation expenses

Repair and depreciation expenses include :

(i) Repair of plant, machinery, building etc.
(ii) Depreciation due to wear and tear, lapse of time and exhaustion of assets used in business.

(e) Miscellaneous expenses

Miscellaneous expenses include :

(i) Loss on the sale of fixed assets
(ii) Loss of goods by fire, theft or accident (not covered by insurance).
(iii) Donation/charity.
(iv) Fines and penalties.

2. Items to the shown on the credit side of profit and loss account

The items of income and gains to be shown on the credit side of profit and loss account are given below :

(i) Discount received
(ii) Commission received
(iii) Rent received
(iv) Interest received
(v) Interest or income from investments
(vi) Bad debits recovered
(vii) Profit on sale of assets
(viii) Miscellaneous receipts

Expenses not to be shown in profit and loss account

The following expenses are not shown in profit and loss account :

(i) Domestic and household expenses

Domestic and household expenses are not shown in profit and loss account, as they are personal expenses of the proprietor and should be treated as drawings.

(ii) Income tax

Income tax paid should not be shown as an expense in profit and loss account but should be treated as personal expense of the proprietor and added to drawings account.

(iii) Life insurance premium

Premium paid on life insurance policy of the proprietor should not be shown as an expense in profit and loss account but should be added to the drawing account.

Balance sheet

Balance sheet may be defined as a statement showing the financial position of a business on a certain fixed date or at the close of the accounting period. It gives information regarding assets and liabilities of the business on any particular date. It is not an account but merely a statement and therefore it has no debit side or credit side, however on its right hand side are written all the left over items of the trial balance. In a common man's language they are called assets e.g. land and building, plant and machinery, furniture and fixtures, goodwill (Pagree), motor vehicles, closing inventory, sundry debtors (the persons from whom money is to be received for credit sales made to him), cash is hand, cash in bank etc. i.e. all those things which the business owns on that particular day and which have a realizable value. On the left hand side of the balance sheet are shown the liabilities of the business including the amount due to the proprietors e.g. capital, loans, creditors for expenses, bills payable, sundry creditors etc. After preparing the balance sheet, if the assets side is bigger the business shows profit but if liabilities side is bigger the business shows loss. A specimen of balance sheet is given below :

Balance Sheet of X.Y.Z. as on 31st March, 1996

Liabilities	Amount Rs.	Assets	Amount Rs.
Ram's capital	15000	Land & building	20000
Sham's capital	10000	Plant & machinery	10000
Loans	25000	Furniture	8000
Sundry creditors	8000	Stores	5000
Bills payable	6000	Vehicles	18000

Continued

Liabilities	Amount Rs.	Assets	Amount Rs.
		Sundry debtors	2000
		Cash in hand	250
		Cash in bank	750
	64000		64000

Advantages of balance sheet

Balance sheet is one of the most important statements prepared in business. It has the following advantages :

(i) It provides information that how much money is invested in the business enterprise.

(ii) It provides information regarding the financial state of the business on a particular date.

(iii) It provides information about the nature and cost of assets of the firm.

(iv) It provides information regarding the nature and amount of liabilities.

(v) It provides information about the capital contributed by the owners.

Since the balance sheet shows the financial position of the enterprise at a glance so the persons like bankers, moneylenders and creditors etc. would like to see the balance sheet of the firm before making any financial deal with the firm to know the financial worthiness of the business.

CLASSIFICATION OF ASSETS AND LIABILITIES

Assets

Assets are the property and possessions of a business which include land, building, plant and machinery, furniture and fixtures, motor vehicles, cash in hand, cash in bank etc. i.e. all those things which the business owns on that particular day and which have a realizable value. The assets are classified according to their nature. Various types of assets are given below :

1. Fixed assets

Fixed assets are those assets which are acquired and held permanently or on long-term basis in the business and are used for the purpose of earning profits. The examples of fixed assets include land, building, plant and machinery, furniture and fixture etc.

2. Current assets (floating assets)

Current assets are those assets which are available either in cash or can be easily converted into cash within a short time to discharge liabilities. The examples of current assets include cash in hand, cash in bank, debtors, stock, bills receivable etc.

3. Tangible assets

Tangible assets are those assets which can be seen and touched. The examples of tangible assets include machinery, cash, stock etc.

4. Intangible assets

Intangible assets are those assets which cannot be seen and touched but have value. The examples of intangible assets include goodwill, patents and trademarks.

5. Fictitious assets

Fictitious assets are fictitious in nature i.e. they are virtually not assets. These are accumulated losses or expenses which are carried forward from one period to the next. The examples of fictitious assets include profit and loss account (debit balance), organisation expenses, discount on the issue of shares, advertisement expenses capitalised from time to time.

6. Wasting assets

Wasting assets are those assets which go on exhausting or reduce in value by their working. The examples of wasting assets include mines and quarries, plant and machinery due to wear and tear.

7. Liquid assets

Liquid assets are those assets which can be converted into cash quickly. Exampies of liquid assets include cash, gold, jewellery, cash certificates etc.

Liabilities

A liability is an amount which a business is legally bound to pay as and when claimed by an outsider on the assets of a business. The liabilities are classified as follows :

1. Fixed liabilities

Fixed liabilities are those liabilities which are payable only on the termination of the business.

2. Long-term liabilities

Long-term liabilities are those liabilities which are payable in future but not within the next accounting period. Examples of long-term liabilities include loans which are repayable after a period of more than one year, debentures etc.

3. Current liabilities

Current liabilities are those liabilities which are expected to be cleared out of current assets within the next accounting period, usually one year or already due. Examples of current liabilities include bank loan, overdraft, rent, taxes, bills payable, payment to creditors etc.

4. Contingent liabilities

Contingent liabilities are those liabilities which are not the actual liabilities but become actual one on the happening of some event which is uncertain and the amount involved is also uncertain. Examples of contingent liabilities include possible penalties, fines or damages from pending litigation, possible assessment of additional taxes, possible payments from default on debits which the company has guaranteed, possible additional payments to employees etc.

Contingent liabilities are not recorded in the balance sheet but they must be disclosed in a footnote.

Difference between Trial Balance and Balance Sheet

S. No.	Point of difference	Trial balance	Balance sheet
1.	Purpose	It is prepared just to check the arithmetical accuracy of the accounts.	It is prepared to know the financial position of the business.
2.	Option	It may or may not be prepared.	It must be prepared as it gives the accurate picture of the business.
3.	Period	It is prepared periodically i.e. fortnightly or monthly.	It is prepared at the close of the accounting period which is generally one year.
4.	Heading	Heading is written as 'Dr' and 'Cr'.	Heading is written as 'Assets' and 'Liabilities'.
5.	Showing profit or loss	It does not show profit or loss.	It shows profit or loss.
6.	Closing stock	Closing stock is not included.	Closing stock is included.
7.	Side of the proforma	Dr is written on the left hand side and Cr is written on the right hand side.	Assets are written on the right hand side and liabilities are written on the left hand side.

Difference between Profit and Loss Account and Balance Sheet

S. No.	Profit and Loss Account	Balance Sheet
1.	In this account the nominal accounts are shown.	Here personal accounts and real accounts are shown.
2.	It provides information regarding net profit or net loss.	It provides information regarding financial position of the business.
3.	It is a ledger account which provides information about debits and credits.	It is only a statement of assets and liabilities.
4.	It is prepared in a bound book.	It is prepared on loose sheets.
5.	It is an account so the words "To" and "By" are used.	It is a statement so the words "To" and "By" are not used.
6.	The balance of this account indicates profit or loss to the business.	The totals on both sides of the balance sheet are always equal.
7.	It is prepared at the end of financial year of the business.	It is prepared on the last date of the financial year under review.

REVISION QUESTIONS

(A) Objective type questions

Put ✓ for correct answer and ✗ for wrong answer in the respective squares given below :

1. Trading and profit and loss account is prepared as on a particular date.
2. Final accounts are prepared at the end of accounting period.
3. Direct expenses relating to the business are transferred to the balance sheet.
4. Indirect expenses relating to the business are transferred to profit and loss account.
5. Wages and salaries are debited to trading account.
6. Gross profit may be less than or more than net profit.
7. Balance sheet is prepared for a particular year.

1	2	3	4	5	6	7

(B) Short-answer type questions

1. Write short notes on the following :
   (i) Financial statements
   (ii) Advantages of financial statements
   (iii) Profit and loss account (iv) Balance sheet
2. Differentiate the following :
   (i) Trading account and profit and loss account.
   (ii) Balance sheet and trial balance.

(C) Long-answer type questions

1. What do you understand from the term 'financial statements'? Describe the advantages and limitations of financial statements.
2. What is profit and loss account? What is the object of preparing profit and loss account? Discuss how it is prepared.
3. What is a balance sheet? Describe the necessity of preparing a balance sheet. Give a proforma of balance sheet.
4. What is the procedure of making a balance sheet? What are the accounts that appear in the balance sheet?

Answers

(A)

1	2	3	4	5	6	7
✗	✓	✗	✓	✓	✗	✗

13

Analysis of Financial Statements or Ratio Analysis

ANALYSIS OF FINANCIAL STATEMENTS

Before discussing the analysis of financial statements one must know that what are financial statements. Financial statements are those statements which are prepared periodically i.e. at the end of the year and all the information recorded in the books of accounts is summarised in these statements. There are two financial statements i.e.

(i) Position statement (balance sheet)

(ii) Income statement (profit and loss statement).

The balance sheet shows the financial position of the company on a given date and profit and loss statements show the profitability of the company.

Analysis of financial statements means the systematic classification, comparison and examination of the facts and figures as disclosed in the statements in order to have full knowledge regarding the profitability and financial position of the company.

TYPE OF FINANCIAL ANALYSIS

Financial analysis is classified into two main categories :

(A) According to the persons interested in such analysis.

(B) According to the methods of operation.

(A) According to the persons interested in such analysis

(i) External analysis

External analysis of financial statements is made by persons like the prospective investors, credit agencies and by the outsiders who have no access to records of the business and who have to depend on the financial statements made available to the outsiders.

(ii) Internal analysis

Internal analysis is made by the executives and employees of the organisation, by the government agencies and courts etc. who have full access to the records of the business and who know full story behind each and every figure in the financial statements.

(B) According to the methods of operations

(i) Dynamic analysis or analysis pertaining to different years

When financial statement of one year is compared to that of other years it is known as dynamic analysis.

(ii) Static or constant analysis

When figures of only one particular year are considered it is known as static or constant analysis.

TECHNIQUES, TOOLS OR METHODS OF FINANCIAL ANALYSIS

The following methods of financial analysis are generally used :

(i) Comparative financial statements
(ii) Common size financial statements
(iii) Funds flow analysis
(iv) Ratio analysis

(i) Comparative financial statements

According to comparative financial statements, the comparative statements of two or more years are prepared to show absolute data of two or more years, increases or decreases in absolute data in value and in terms of percentages.

Comparative statements can be prepared for profit and loss account as well as balance sheet. The profit and loss statement discloses the net profit or net loss resulting from the operation of balance. Comparative balance sheet discloses any increase or decrease of assets and liabilities of the company.

Now-a-days a number of companies publish year to year comparative financial statements giving figures and information at least for the current year and the previous year.

(ii) Common size financial statements (common measurement analysis)

In common size statements the figures reported in income statement and balance sheet are converted into percentage to some common base e.g. in income statement the sale figure is taken as base and all other figures are expressed as percentage of sales. Similarly in the balance sheet the total of assets and liabilities is taken as base and all other figures are expressed as percentage of this total. The percentage so calculated can be easily compared with the corresponding percentages in other periods and useful conclusions can be drawn.

(iii) Funds flow analysis

Here "Funds" means the working capital and "Fund flow" means change in funds or change in working capital. In other words increase or decrease in working capital is known as "flow of funds".

Funds flow statement is prepared to know the sources from where the working capital was obtained and the purpose for which it is used during the accounting period.

(iv) Ratio analysis

Ratio analysis is the most popular method of analysis of financial statements because it is simple and more informative. A ratio is an arithmetical relationship between two figures. For example if total sales is Rs. 36,00,000 and the gross profit is Rs. 9,00,000, then the gross profit in terms of ratio will be :

$$\frac{9,00,000}{36,00,000} \times 100 = 25\% \text{ of sales}$$

This is the ratio or relationship between gross profit and sales.

The ratios are valuable but they alone do not convey any meaning unless compared with a similar ratio of the past or of a similar firm which gives a useful relationship to know the performance and financial position of the enterprise.

Importance or advantages of ratio analysis

The ratio analysis has the following advantages :

1. It is helpful to the management that a number of important decisions concerning planning and forecasting can be taken. The ratio may also be helpful in making any change in the organisation structure.
2. Ratio analysis provides the information regarding financial position of the enterprise which is very helpful to the banks, insurance companies, other financial institutions and any other person who is concerned with the business of the company.
3. It is helpful to the investors because they would like to invest in the company only if the company pays a good rate of dividend to the shareholders.
4. It is helpful to the employees that they can come to know the profitability of the business on the basis of which they can demand higher pay and bonus etc.
5. It is helpful to the creditors that by judging the financial position of the company they may supply the goods on credit.
6. It is helpful to the government because on the information provided by the business houses the government can take certain policy-making decisions regarding the industries.
7. It is useful for making comparison of progress made by one company with the progress made by other company

Limitations of ratio analysis

Ratio analysis has the following limitations :

1. The ratio does not show the exact position of the business. The exact position can only be known if the business is closed.
2. Ratio is based on the given financial statements. If the information

provided in the financial statements is not proper then the ratio will definitely be misleading.

3. The comparison between different firms is difficult because different firms use different methods for calculating the value of stock and for charging depreciation.
4. Ratio analysis is one of the most important methods of analysis of financial statements. They provide only a fraction of information needed for decision-making. So to get a thorough analysis of financial statements, ratio analysis should be used along with other methods of analysis.

Classification of ratios

Various ratios may be classified as follows :

1. Profitability ratios
2. Liquidity ratios
3. Activity ratios
4. Long-term solvency ratios

1. Profitability ratios

Profitability ratios are of great importance for a business enterprise. These ratios are calculated to know the end results of the business activity. The various ratios covered under profitability ratios are as follows :

(a) Gross profit ratio

Gross profit ratio tells us the gross margin on trading which is calculated as follows :

$$\text{Gross profit ratio} = \frac{\text{Gross profit}}{\text{Net sales}} \times 100$$

(b) Net profit ratio

Net profit ratio is also known as net profit margin. It is the relationship between the net profit and net sales of the business. It is calculated as under :

$$\text{Net profit ratio} = \frac{\text{Net profit}}{\text{Net sales}} \times 100$$

(c) Operating profit ratio

It is the relationship between operating profit and net sales which is calculated as follows :

$$\text{Operating profit ratio} = \frac{\text{Operating profit}}{\text{Net sales}} \times 100$$

(d) Return of capital employed ratio

This ratio establishes the relationship between the earnings and the capital employed in the business. It is calculated as follows :

$$\text{Return on capital employed} = \frac{\text{Net profit}}{\text{Capital employed}} \times 100$$

(e) Return on total assets ratio

This ratio is calculated to measure the profit after tax against the amount invested in total assets to know whether assets are being utilized properly or not. This ratio is calculated as follows :

$$\text{Return on total assets} = \frac{\text{Net profit after tax}}{\text{Total assets}} \times 100$$

(b) Payout ratio

This ratio is used to determine that what proportion of earnings per share has been used for paying dividends and what has been retained for ploughing back. This ratio is very important from shareholders' point of view. This ratio is determined as follows :

$$\text{Payout ratio} = \frac{\text{Dividend per equity share}}{\text{Earning per share}}$$

The other ratios are calculated as follows :

(g) $$\text{Earning per share} = \frac{\text{Net profit after tax}}{\text{Total number of shares}} \times 100$$

(h) $$\text{Dividend per share} = \frac{\text{Total amount paid to shareholders}}{\text{Outstanding number of shares}}$$

(i) $$\text{Dividend yield ratio} = \frac{\text{Dividend per share}}{\text{Market value of share}}$$

(j) $$\text{Earning yield ratio} = \frac{\text{Earning per share}}{\text{Market value of share}}$$

2. Liquidity ratios

Liquidity ratios are used to measure the ability of the concern to pay off its liabilities in time. The following ratios are used to calculate the short-term solvency position of the firm :

(a) Current ratio
(b) Liquid ratio

(a) Current ratio

It is also known as working capital ratio. This ratio expresses the relationship between the current assets and current liabilities. This is the most widely used ratio by the business concerns and commercial banks to know the short-term solvency of the business. Current ratio is calculated as follows :

$$\text{Current ratio} = \frac{\text{Current assets}}{\text{Current liabilities}}$$

(b) Liquid ratio

Liquid ratio is also known as acid test ratio or quick ratio. Liquid ratio is an improvement over the current ratio because here the liquid assets are taken into consideration.

Liquid assets are those assets which can be converted into cash within a short period without any loss in value. Liquid assets include bank balances, securities and debtors. Liquid ratio is calculated as follows :

$$\text{Liquid ratio} = \frac{\text{Liquid assets}}{\text{Current liabilities}}$$

3. Activity ratios

Activity ratios are also known as turnover ratios or efficiency ratios. These ratios are used to measure the efficiency with which the firm uses its resources or assets. The speed with which the assets are used indicates the efficiency of the business organisation. Some of the important turnover ratios are given below :

(a) Inventory turnover ratio (ITR)

(b) Capital turnover ratio

(a) Inventory turnover ratio

Inventory turnover ratio is also known as stock turnover ratio. It is used to know that how many times the company's average stock is being converted into sales. A high inventory turnover ratio indicates the efficient management of the inventory whereas low inventory turnover ratio indicates the inefficient management of the inventory. Thus a firm should have a proper inventory turnover. Inventory turnover ratio can be calculated from the following formula :

$$\text{Inventory turnover ratio} = \frac{\text{Cost of goods sold}}{\text{Average stock}}$$

where

Cost of goods sold = Net sales – Gross profit

Net sales = Total sales – Returns inward

Total sales = Cash sales + Credit sales

$$\text{Average stock} = \frac{\text{Opening stock} + \text{Closing stock}}{2}$$

(b) Capital turnover ratio

Capital turnover ratio is used to measure the relationship between the sales and the capital employed in the business. It is calculated as follows :

$$\text{Capital turnover} = \frac{\text{Sales}}{\text{Capital employed}}$$

4. Long-term solvency ratios

Solvency ratio is also known as leverage ratio. Solvency means the liabilities as and when they mature for payment. These ratios are calculated to see whether the business concern would be able to meet its long-term commitments i.e. the ability of the firm to pay regularly interest due on long-term loans as well as the payment of the principal amount. Generally long-term creditors like debenture holders and the suppliers of fixed assets on instalment basis are interested in solvency ratios. The solvency is measured from the following ratios :

(a) Debt equity ratio
(b) Debt to total capital ratio

(a) Debt equity ratio or external internal equities ratio

It is used to measure relative claims of creditors and owners of the firm. It is calculated as follows :

$$\text{Debt equity ratio} = \frac{\text{Long–term debt}}{\text{Shareholders' equity}}$$

$$\text{or} \qquad = \frac{\text{External equities}}{\text{Internal equities}}$$

$$\text{or} \qquad = \frac{\text{Outsiders' funds}}{\text{Insiders' funds}}$$

where

Shareholders' equity = Equity share capital + Surplus + Preference share capital

This ratio is an important ratio by which the financial structure of the company can be evaluated. A high debt equity ratio means the shareholders' claim in the company is low whereas a low debt equity ratio shows a higher claims of shareholders in the company.

(b) Debit to total capital ratio

This ratio is used to find out the relationship between long-term debt and total capital which can be calculated as follows :

$$\text{Debt to total capital} = \frac{\text{Long–term debt}}{\text{Total capital}}$$

where

Total capital = Shareholders' funds + Long-term debts

Lower the debt to total capital ratio, better will be the long-term solvency position of the business and higher the debt to total capital ratio, low will be the long-term solvency position of the business.

REVISION QUESTIONS

(A) Very-short answer type questions

Define the following .

(i) Ratio analysis (ii) Current ratio
(iii) Liquidity ratio (iv) Solvency ratio
(v) Gross profit ratio (vi) Net profit ratio

(B) Short-answer type questions

1. Describe the advantages and disadvantages of financial analysis.
2. Enumerate various ratios used in ratio analysis.

3. Discuss various methods of financial analysis.

(C) Long-answer type questions

1. What do you understand from analysis of financial statements? Discuss various methods used for financial analysis.
2. What is ratio analysis? Describe advantages and disadvantages of ratio analysis.
3. Describe various ratio analyses used for analysing the financial statements.

14

Budgeting

In the chapter of financial statements we have seen that the analysis of financial statements is of great importance in judging the past operations and the present financial position of the business. But for the future progress of the business it is very important to plan and control the activities of the business which is done through budgets.

Budget planning starts with the setting up of an object to be achieved by a business during the next budget period, say the next twelve months.

A budget is a detailed plan of operations for some specific future period. It is an estimate prepared in advance of the period to which it applies. The management of all the concerns want that all operations should be forecast and as far as possible the objectives set aside for that period are fulfilled.

A budget is essential in all walks of our life i.e. national, business and domestic. Even the housewife prepares a budget for the whole month and according to that budget she spends the money. A budget is prepared to have effective utilization of funds for the realisation of objectives as efficiently as possible. The Institute of Cost and Management Accounts, England defines a budget as under :

"A financial and/or quantitative statement, prepared and approved prior to a defined period of time, of the policy to be pursued during that period for the purpose of attaining a given objective."

Essential of a budget

(i) It is prepared in advance for future plan of action.

(ii) It is prepared for definite future period.

(iii) It is prepared to achieve the objectives set for the definite future period.

(iv) It is a statement expressed in monetary and/or physical units prepared for the implementation of policies framed by the management.

Budgetary control

The Institute of Cost and Management Accountants, England has defined budgetary control as :

"The establishment of budgets relating the responsibilities of executives to the requirements of a policy, and the continuous comparison of actual with budgeted results, either to secure by individual action the objectives of that policy or to provide a firm basis for its revision."

In short, budgetary control means laying down in monetary and quantitative terms what exactly has to be done, at what time it is to be done and how it is to be done so as to achieve the actual results according to the planned programmes.

Difference between budget, budgeting and budgetary control

The differences between budget, budgeting and budgetary control are explained by Rowland and William as follows :

"Budgets are the individual objectives of a department, etc. whereas budgeting may be said to be the act of building budgets. Budgetary control embraces all this and in addition includes the science of planning the budgets themselves and the utilisation of such budgets to effect an overall management tool for the business planning and control."

Objectives of budgetary control

The main objectives of budgetary control are given below :

1. Planning
2. Co-ordination
3. Control

1. Planning

A sound planning is necessary for the success of any firm. So it is very essential to prepare the budget and draw the detailed programmes relating to production schedule, raw material costs, sales targets, research programmes, advertising programmes etc. The budgetary control will force the management at all levels to plan in time all the activities to be done during the future periods.

2. Co-ordination

For effective planning and implementation co-ordination between different departments and managements is very necessary. Budget control helps to co-ordinate the various activities of the firm and secure co-operation of all concerned so that the common objectives of the firm may be successfully achieved.

3. Control

Control is necessary to ensure that all the plans and objectives are implemented and achieved successfully. This is only possible through budgetary control which makes control possible by comparing the actual performance with pre-determined plans and objectives and reporting the shortcomings to the management for corrective action.

Advantages of budgetary control

Budgetary control has the following advantages :

(i) It brings co-ordination between different departments of the firm.

(ii) It brings efficiency in the working of business enterprise.

(iii) It decreases the wastage and losses to a great extend thus brings economy to the enterprise.

(iv) It establishes individual responsibilities, therefore, everyone knows what is to be done and at what time it is to be done to achieve the targets of the enterprise.

(v) There is no delay in any kind of work since budgets are prepared before hand and act as sanction to do the work.

(vi) It checks undue expenditure because the targets are fixed by the executives of the firm after giving due consideration to every aspect of business. Thus it keeps the working capital within limits according to the requirements of the business.

(vii) The actual results achieved can be compared with the budgetary provisions and weak points can be appropriately handled to achieve the targets.

(viii) Well-planned and target-oriented budgets receive greater favour from credit agencies and financial institutions.

(ix) It helps in the purchase of stores which is based on the pre-determined requirements for raw materials thus prevents stock shortages, as well as excessive purchases.

Limitations of budgetary control

Though all kinds of precautions are taken while preparing the budget even then some deficiencies do arise. So budgeting is not a fool-proof tool. It has the following limitations :

(i) Too much time is spent in the preparation of budgets.

(ii) Experts and technical persons are required for preparing the budgets.

(iii) It requires teamwork and proper cooperation of top management and coordination among different departments.

(iv) It is very difficult to prepare an accurate budget depending on future predictions. Moreover government policies go on changing from time to time due to which the accurate position of the business cannot be estimated.

(v) There is always positive and negative reaction to budgetary control because it points out efficiency and inefficiency of individual workers and management. The opposition is mainly due to human nature—the tendency to resist change. So any system of budgetary control cannot be successful unless it has the full support of top management and cooperation of workers.

Though budgetary control has certain limitations but budgetary control is must for the success of any business enterprise. The enterprise can achieve a great success if budgets are prepared by experts after giving due consideration to every aspect of business and top management and workers give full cooperation for the successful implementation of budgetary control programmes.

Classification of budgets

Basic classification of budgets are as follows :

1. Classification according to time factor.
2. Classification according to flexibility factor.
3. Functional classification.

1. Classification according to time factor

According to time factor the budgets are classified as follows :

(i) Long-term budgets

Long-term budgets are prepared for long-term planning and operations of the firm. Such budgets are prepared for a period varying from 5 to 10 years.

(ii) Short-term budgets

Short-term budgets are prepared for short periods only i.e. only for one or two years.

(iii) Current budgets

Current budgets are prepared according to the current conditions or prevailing circumstances of the firm. Such budgets are prepared for a month or so.

2. Classification according to flexibility factor

According to flexibility factor the budget can be classified as follows :

(i) Fixed budgets

Fixed budgets are those budgets which are prepared on the basis of a statement or fixed level of activity. In fixed budgets the targets are rigidly fixed and do not change with the change in activity. Such budgets are generally prepared one to three months in advance of the year to which it pertains. Fixed budget has a number of limitations so it is ineffective as a tool for cost control.

(ii) Flexible budgets

Flexible budgets are those budgets which are subject to change in accordance with the level of activity actually attained. Flexible budgets permit easy adjustments of the budgets according to changed business conditions. So this type of budget is more elastic, useful and practical.

3. Functional classification

Functional budgets are those budgets which relate to various functions of a firm. There are a number of individual budgets which vary from firm to firm but the following functional budgets are commonly used :

(i) Sales budget

(ii) Production budget

  (a) Raw material budget

  (b) Labour budget

  (c) Plan utilisation budget

(iii) Purchase budget

(iv) Capital expenditure budget

(v) Administrative expenses budget

(vi) Research and development budget

(vii) Cash budget

(viii) Master budget

(i) Sales budget

The sales budget is the most important budget and forms the basis on which all the other budgets are prepared. This budget is a forecast of the quantities and values of sales to be achieved in a budget period. The sales manager is responsible for the preparation and execution of this budget. In the preparation of sales budget the sales manager may take into consideration past sales, market conditions, advertisements, competitions and new developments etc.

The sales budget is prepared in terms of quantities and amounts and the sales estimates must be analysed for products, periods and territories. The sales budget should include an estimate of selling and distribution costs in addition to an estimate of the total sales.

(ii) Production budget

The sales estimate will show the amount of each product required from time to time. The purpose of the production budget is to ensure regular supply of each item to meet the demand of the sales department. The production budget determines the quantities of each item in stock, what is required to be produced, at what time it is to be produced, how it is to be produced and where it is to be produced. Production budget should be prepared in such a way that the stock on hand should not become too large which may lead to financial losses due to many reasons such as deterioration, changes in style, spoilage and storage charges but at the same time the stock should not become too small which may lead to low sales or no sales because no goods will be available for sale. The responsibility for the preparation of production budget lies with the works manager.

(a) Raw materials budget

Once it is determined that how much quantity of any product is to be produced then it becomes necessary to lay down the requirements of raw materials. It should be known that what kind of raw material and in what quantity it is required. For example in the preparation of B-complex capsules different kinds of vitamins, excipients and capsule shells are required. The quantity of each raw material depends on the total quantity of capsules to be prepared.

(b) Labour budget

Labour budget is very important because it determines the labour force required to complete any work. If a job requires more time for its completion then the labour force can be increased. Similarly in the lean periods or off seasons the labour force can be decreased.

(c) Plan utilisation budget

The requirement of machines in a manufacturing house are carefully determined. They must be according to the requirement. A production manager must ensure that all the machines are fully utilized and production plans are so worked out that at no time any machine should remain unutilised.

(iii) Purchase budget

Purchase budgets are extremely important because it is directly associated with the production budget. Purchase budgets for the purchase of raw materials, spare parts and machines are prepared on monthly, half yearly and yearly basis. The materials are purchased according to economic order quantity basis and on the affordable lowest market price without any compromise with the quality of the materials. Purchase budgets should be prepared in such a way that the required materials are purchased at appropriate time without affecting the production schedule.

(iv) Capital expenditure budget

Capital expenditure budget is prepared to know the approximate amount of capital needed for acquiring the fixed assets in the budget period. Capital may be needed for additions, alterations or replacement of old machines with an improved type of machines so as to reduce cost of production. To ensure the availability of capital at the right time and to prevent disruption in the normal working of an enterprise this budget is prepared to plan the future expenditure over the budgeting periods. Thus capital expenditure budget helps to know what new assets are needed and at what time.

(v) Administrative expenses budget

Administrative expenses budget provides an estimate of the expenses incurred in controlling the business operations which include expenses of all administrative offices and of management salaries. The budget can be prepared with the help of past experience and anticipated charges. This budget is prepared for each department which is then totalled to get the budget for the entire administrative division.

(vi) Research and development budget

All the big manufacturing houses and business organisations allot a separate budget every year for research and development work to find new products and to find new methods so as to make improvement in the quality of existing products. This budget is prepared taking into consideration the research projects in hand and the new projects to be taken up. Thus the research and development budget provides an estimate of the expenditure to be incurred on research and development during the budget period.

(vii) Cash budget

Cash budget is also known as financial budget which is very important for any business organisation because it commands all other budgets. This budget gives an estimate of all possible cash receipts and payments during the budget period. It is prepared for the guidance of the management so that arrangements may be made with the bank to provide the necessary finance to meet the production and sales programmes of the organisation. Cash budget also provides knowledge if any surplus cash is available which may be invested to earn some higher income. Purchase of materials or goods is also facilitated by this budget.

(viii) Master budget or final budget

The master budget is a consolidated summary of the various functional budgets. When the functional budgets are completed by different departments, they are sent to the budget officer who compiles all the budgets to prepare a master budget.

The budget committee approves the master budget which becomes the target for the company during the budget period.

The master budget generally contains details regarding sales, production costs, cash position and key account balances such as fixed assets, bills payable, debtors, stock etc.

REVISION QUESTIONS

(A) Very-short answer type questions

Define the following :

(i) Budget
(ii) Budgeting control
(iii) Budget period

(B) Short-answer type questions

Write short notes on the following :

(i) Budgeting control
(ii) Objectives of budgetary control
(iii) Long-term budgets
(iv) Short-term budgets
(v) Current budgets
(vi) Master budgets
(vii) Advantages of budgeting
(viii) Limitations of budgeting

(C) Long-answer type questions

1. Explain the term 'budgetary control'. Describe advantages and limitations of budgetary control.
2. What do you understand from the terms 'budget' and 'budgetary control'? Describe the objectives and limitations of budgetary control.
3. What is a budget? Classify the budgets and explain the functional budgets in detail.
4. Write short notes on the following :
   (a) Fixed budget
   (b) Flexible budget
   (c) Sales budget
   (d) Production budget
   (e) Purchase budget
   (f) Cash budget
   (g) Labour budget

Index